To my dearest Dec

With

love.

Moni

Happy New Year. 1988.

Stillwater Trout

Stillwater Trout
Tackle and Techniques

JOHN MITCHELL

PELHAM BOOKS

First published in Great Britain by
Pelham Books Ltd
27 Wrights Lane
London W8 5TZ
1987

All the photographs are the copyright
of the author unless otherwise credited.
Line drawings by Marg Howdle.

British Library Cataloguing in Publication Data
Mitchell, John E.
   Stillwater trout: tackle and techniques.
   1. Trout fishing
   I. Title
   799.1'755   SH687
   ISBN 0-7207-1787-6

Typeset by Goodfellow & Egan (Phototypesetting) Ltd, Cambridge
Printed and bound in Great Britain by Butler & Tanner Ltd, Frome

Contents

To Harold who started it all

Acknowledgements

My thanks firstly to the late Jack Harrigan, former holder of the British Barbel Record, and proprietor of Judds of Hillingdon who introduced me to the tackle trade. Also to Fred Jarvis of EMAP National Publications who had sufficient faith to employ me as advertisement manager of *Sea Angler* and *Sporting Gun* where I made many friends in the tackle trade. Thanks also to Omri Thomas, managing director of Normark Sport Ltd, for his unstinting help and advice.

My grateful thanks to *Trout Fisherman* magazine for their permission to use excerpts from some of my articles previously published by them, and to the members of Kennick Flyfishers who have helped to make my fishing so enjoyable over the last few years.

Finally, my thanks to my wife Linda who has spent many hours on the banks of various stillwater fisheries sometimes fishing, sometimes waiting for me. I hope that this makes it all worth while.

Introduction

It is often said that 25 per cent of the anglers catch 75 per cent of the fish. In terms of stillwater trout fishing this means that 25 per cent of anglers are being subsidised by the rest. It also means that 75 per cent of the anglers are not getting their fair share, and perhaps are not enjoying and benefiting from their sport as much as they might.

Whilst there will always be good and poor anglers, any angler who increases his knowledge of his quarry, tackle and angling methods can improve the standard of his fishing, and get more enjoyment and satisfaction from his sport.

The aim of this book is to impart that information, and if one angler enjoys more success as a result of reading it, the book will have served its purpose. A good angler is a happy angler who can instil his enthusiasm in others. The more successful anglers we have, the better our fisheries will become.

The demand for good quality fishing will dictate the future of our sport. Whether we fish water authority reservoirs or private put-and-take fisheries, the management and owners are responsible for providing top quality sport. As the demand increases, the number of fisheries will increase. Competition is healthy, and we the anglers will benefit in the long term.

Above all, let us remember that stillwater trout fishing is a 'sport for all'.

Chapter 1

The fish we catch

Both the rainbow trout and the brown trout are members of the salmon family (*Salmonidae*). They have an additional fin between the dorsal fin and the tail called the adipose fin. This together with the lack of scales on the head is the only external physical difference between game fish and coarse fish. The other major difference is that the salmon family spawn in the winter, whereas all coarse fish spawn in the spring. The close season for trout fishing therefore runs from October to March in most areas, and the close season for coarse fish runs from mid-March to mid-June.

Fishing for rainbow trout may continue all year as they do not breed naturally in the United Kingdom, but any brown trout caught out of season must be returned to the water. Fisheries which open throughout the year usually stock with sterile fish during the winter in order that anglers can catch fish in prime condition rather than fish suffering from the ravages of a frustrated breeding season.

Rainbow trout

The rainbow trout, the stillwater angler's usual quarry, was originally introduced from America just before the turn of the century. The rainbow grows faster than our native brown trout, and is therefore a more economic and efficient proposition for the many fish farms now dotted about the countryside. The rainbow trout converts a much greater percentage of its food to weight, and weight is the main criterion by which anglers judge their catch. It is also generally accepted that the rainbow is easier to catch than the brown trout.

If anglers relied on natural brown trout replenishment, or put-and-take policies based on brown trout, the cost of fishing would rise, and the average weight of fish would fall.

The rainbow trout (*Salmo gairdneri*) can be divided into two subspecies:

1. *Salmo gairdneri irideus* is a migratory rainbow trout commonly known in America as the steelhead. It can be compared with our own sea trout. They feed substantially at sea, but have to return to fresh water to breed. They can be stocked in lakes, but there is no chance of them breeding. The *irideus* breeds in late winter or spring, depending on the temperature of the

water. It is therefore not so popular with fishery managers, as after a cold winter the fish may be very much out of condition at the opening of the season. The very dark (black) rainbows caught in April and early May will probably be *irideus* rainbows or *irideus/shasta* hybrids.

2. *Salmo gairdneri shasta* is a non-migratory rainbow trout which commonly breeds in the autumn. This is the favourite fish of stillwater fishery owners due to the fact that anglers do not mind catching a late-season fish with roe in it. Hopefully, by the opening day of the season the *shasta* rainbow will be fully recovered from spawning albeit artificial, and will both look and fight well for the angler. The *shasta* rainbow, being non-migratory, can breed naturally in the United Kingdom, but not in still water. There are records of them breeding in the River Chess, and rumours of them breeding in the Test. However, it is unlikely that natural breeding will become widespread in this country.

The two subspecies can be interbred (hybridised) readily, but difficulties can occur due to the different breeding seasons which only overlap for a short period. Both subspecies and hybrids grow and mature much faster than the brown trout, but do not live as long. The maximum life of a rainbow is about seven years, whereas a brown trout can live for over twenty years. There are

A perfect 3 lb 9 oz rainbow trout.

however records of rainbow trout weighing over 45 lb in the USA, and the largest authenticated rainbow caught in the UK weighed 21 lb 4 oz.

The majority of rainbow trout stocked in our stillwater fisheries are females; they can be identified by the receding lower jaw. The female rainbow does not darken as rapidly with the onset of the spawning season, and they recover from spawning more quickly than the male. It has also been established that there can be a very high mortality of male rainbows left to over-winter in a fishery, whereas a larger proportion of the female fish survive.

We must take for granted the fact that all the rainbow trout we catch are reared on fish farms. The rearing process is fairly straightforward, but a lot of research has been carried out in order to keep mortality to a minimum, and to produce fast-growing fit fish. In basic terms the milt is stripped from a ripe male fish, and the eggs are stripped from a ripe female fish. The milt and eggs are then mixed together, and the eggs are fertilised by the male sperm. The chief requirement is a steady supply of pure water at a steady temperature of around 10 degrees Centigrade. The eggs are kept in trays with water constantly passing over them. The newly hatched young fish are called alevins, and they initially feed by absorbing their integral yolk sac, after which they are fed artemia which is a very small shrimp. During the last few years artemia has come to be replaced by dry high-protein food.

Feeding fish in the holding cages at Upper Tamar Reservoir.

The fingerling trout are transferred to outdoor stewponds where they are fed on high-protein pellets two or three times a day. A rainbow trout will reach a weight of 1 lb in its first year whereas a brown trout may well be into its third year before attaining this weight. Stewpond rainbows can reach almost 20 lb in three years if fed regularly and kept in a restricted area.

The flesh of a rainbow trout is naturally white. However, the fish farms supplying the consumer market quickly established that the now familiar pink flesh, so similar to that of the sea trout and salmon, was preferable. Carotene pigment found in many crustaceans such as shrimps and prawns was therefore introduced into trout pellets to make the flesh pink. There is nothing wrong with the introduction of carotene – it is a natural product which colours the flesh of sea trout and salmon, plus the brown trout resident in some lochs and lakes. It does not alter the taste of the flesh, but certainly improves its appearance.

Brown trout

The brown trout (*Salmo trutta*) is our native trout. It is found throughout the United Kingdom and most of Europe, and has been introduced to the USA, Australia, Canada, and even parts of Africa. Whilst the rainbow is the main quarry of stillwater anglers, the catching of a brown trout is a bonus. During the last few years a number of anglers have concentrated on catching large brown trout from waters such as Grafham, Rutland, and the Queen Mother

Feeding fish in the stew ponds at Watercress Farm.

Reservoir at Datchet. In waters where food is abundant brown trout can grow to a very good size. They become very carnivorous as they grow larger.

Initially the brown trout was divided into numerous subspecies. The ordinary brown trout was called *Salmo fario*, the sea trout *Salmo eriox*, the lake trout *Salmo lacustris*, and the large lake trout *Salmo ferox*. In some cases, trout from a particular individual lake were given their own Latin name and listed as a subspecies. Large cannibal trout caught in Scottish lochs are still known as Ferox trout. In Ireland they have the local name of Gillaroo, being a large brightly coloured brown trout.

Scientists today regard all varieties of brown trout as *Salmo trutta*, particular differences among trout taken from various waters being attributed to their diverse surroundings or feeding habits. Brown trout breed naturally in both rivers and lakes in the United Kingdom. In still waters benefiting from a stream supply, the brown trout will run up the stream if suitable breeding sites are available. They will however breed on gravel shallows in still water although the mortality rate of the eggs is likely to be greater.

The brown trout can easily be identified by its larger spots which are often red, and the lack of spots on the tail. The male fish sports a jutting lower jaw, which in larger specimens extends into an upward hook (kype) during the breeding season. The brown trout will breed at any time between October and February, the peak

Wild brown trout.
(*Photo: Steve Windsor*)

months being November and December. The eggs hatch in between one and three months depending upon the temperature of the water. The artificial rearing of brown trout is identical to that of rainbows but, as previously mentioned, their growth rate is considerably slower; few brown trout are bred in captivity for this reason.

A large brown trout is a majestic fish, and in order to maintain reasonable stocks of brownies in our still waters it is very necessary to rigidly observe size limits. Very few still waters are stocked with brown trout, and the population is maintained in many reservoirs by natural spawning. If reasonable brown trout are to be caught, it is necessary to return undersized fish to the water unharmed. Where fishery rules permit, it would not be a bad policy to return any brown trout which are under the average size of the resident rainbows. The stock level would consequently be maintained, and the size of the fish would increase.

The brown trout is a dogged fighter. It will bore deep and make long runs. Its flashier cousin, the rainbow, appears to spend half its time in the air after it is hooked, but will usually come to the net quicker than a brownie.

American brook trout

The American brook trout (*Salvelinus fontinalis*) is in fact a char. It is a native of North America and Canada, being a lover of cold water. These fish can grow to a weight of 5–6 lb in American

An American brook trout caught in Colorado USA by Chris Dawn.
(Photo: Chris Dawn)

waters, and stewpond fish have been grown to over 5 lb in the United Kingdom. The average weight however is around 1½ lb. The brook trout has been bred artificially and introduced to a few of our stillwater fisheries, but it is not suitable for small fisheries which experience high water temperatures in summer. It is a highly coloured fish resembling a rainbow trout, the pectoral fins having white leading edges. The American brook trout has been of interest to fish farmers due to its ability to hybridise with other trout and char.

Tiger trout

The tiger trout is a brook trout/brown trout hybrid. It is a sterile fish which is not affected by the ravages of the breeding season, and does not therefore get out of condition. Instead of utilising its food to produce eggs or milt, the tiger trout can convert it into weight. Being sterile, the tiger trout is purely a put-and-take fish, but smaller fisheries find that they can control their stocking policy more efficiently by using these hybrids. Both the brook trout and the tiger trout have the reputation of being easy to catch. They hit a lure hard, and do not appear to be fussy about its appearance.

Cheetah trout

The cheetah trout is a brook trout/rainbow trout hybrid, which is again a sterile fish. The famous Avington fishery did much to

Cheetah trout from Avington. *(Photo: John Wilshaw)*

develop this hybrid which has mottled markings rather than the stripes of the tiger trout. However, little has been heard of either the tiger trout or the cheetah trout, although they are ideal for stocking in smaller fisheries.

It would appear that fish farmers prefer to rely on the rainbow trout because of its faster growth rate. Although the trout/char hybrids have a faster growth rate than brown trout, the smaller size of the char limits their growth to some extent. No doubt demand also plays a large part in influencing the fish farmer as to which species of fish will be more profitable for him, so it may well be up to the fishery owners to be a little more adventurous and try these hybrids for themselves.

Triploids

Whilst hybridisation is one way to produce sterile fish which are fit to catch all the year round, research work over the last few years has led to the development of a sterile rainbow trout commonly known as a triploid. Here, the fish farmer has the best of both worlds – a fast-growing fish capable of attaining very large size and which will maintain its condition throughout the year.

The triploid is produced by feeding the hormone testosterone to breeding stock. This makes both male and female fish produce sperm. The male sperm is discarded, but the female sperm is mixed with normal eggs which when fertilised produce female ova. The eggs are then given sudden heat treatment which almost kills them, and they are then cooled.

In normal eggs, when the nucleus splits there are two chromosomes to each split nucleus, but in the case of triploids there are three chromosomes, which make the fish sterile. The triploid grows very rapidly and there is no doubt that many still waters will stock with these fish in the next few years. Both the South West Water Authority and the Anglian Water Authority have stocked triploids over the last few years. Their growth rate, high winter survival rate, and guaranteed maintenance of good condition make them an economical and efficient fish for the stillwater fishery.

Salmon

One or two privately owned stillwater fisheries have recently introduced salmon, which are now bred commercially in Scotland. Initial results from the different fisheries do not lead us to any definite conclusions regarding this policy, but the fishery owners are to be admired for trying this experiment. Naturally bred salmon do not feed in fresh water after they have returned from the sea, but it is possible that a salmon grown under controlled conditions will feed continuously because it will never have been to the sea. One must however bear in mind that salmon are expensive, and therefore the cost of this type of fishing is higher than that of trout fishing. Notions of catching thirty-pounders are better forgotten.

The foregoing then is the list of fish that we are likely to catch, together with a brief natural history. Other fish such as roach, bream, and carp may take your fly on occasions. Trout anglers treat these as vermin, but please, if fishery rules allow, return them to the water. Perch and pike however can cause havoc in a trout fishery, and it is highly likely that the fishery owners will require these fish to be killed. Some fisheries now open during the close season for coarse fishing, and several have organised pike fishing competitions in order to remove these predators from their waters.

Many anglers ask whether or not rainbow and brown trout conflict with each other in a mixed fishery. In put-and-take fisheries where a high stocking density is maintained, there must be a certain amount of conflict due to the fact that the fish population may well outweigh the food potential of the water. Whilst brown trout are very territorial in streams, they move about more readily in lakes as they have to search for their food. Rainbow trout shoal more readily and are therefore less territorial by nature. If a brown trout maintains a territory it is likely that it will maintain it against rainbows as well as other brown trout.

Since the boom in stillwater trout fishing really got under way in the early 1970s, there has been a lot of controversy regarding British Records. Personally I cannot accept that huge rainbow trout bred in fish farms, raised in stewponds, and stocked into small put-and-take fisheries can be serious contenders for record titles. The fish are not openly available to all anglers, the fishing is purely artificial, and the whole matter of claiming a record is open to abuse and deception.

Regardless of species, surely any fish which does not breed naturally and readily in this country cannot be included in any record fish list published by a nationally recognised angling body. Certainly individual fisheries will have a record fish list, but in reality our stillwater trout fishing *is* artificial and any records relating to fish caught in these fisheries will be artificial to the same extent.

Chapter 2

Stillwater fisheries

Although the trout-fishing boom took place in the 1960s and 1970s, stillwater fisheries have been with us for hundreds of years. The Scottish lochs are the obvious example, and the majority of them rely on natural re-population.

It is the put-and-take fishery which has come to prominence in recent years, but one must remember that Blagdon was open not long after the turn of the century. The Bristol Waterworks Company reared their own rainbow trout and operated a stocking policy long before the water authorities were officially directed to open their reservoirs for leisure activities.

The government directive in the 1960s led to the stillwater trout fishing boom, and at last trout fishing was available to everyone. In former years only anglers living near to lakes holding trout, or members of syndicates, could enjoy the sport. It was obvious to the water authorities that in order to comply with the government directive and make reservoirs available for leisure activities, the easiest thing to do was to stock them with fish, and to charge for the privilege of catching them. There was no need to make a profit on the operation, but hopefully they would break even. This has not necessarily proved to be the case, and recently we have seen the water authorities putting the fishing rights of their reservoirs out to tender in an attempt to reduce staff numbers and overhead expenses.

Naturally enough, the increased demand for rainbow trout led to an increase in the number of fish farms, and business-minded fish-farmers opened their own fisheries. Avington is a prime example. Other landowners with lakes, disused gravel workings, and marshy ground that could be dredged also decided that stillwater trout fishing could produce a good income. Some were right, many were not.

We therefore have a tremendous variation in the types of stillwater fisheries that we can visit, from the natural lochs of Scotland which are in the main unstocked, to natural lakes, reservoirs with natural banks, artificial lakes, gravel pits, ponds, and the concrete bowl reservoirs, all of which are stocked in one form or another. They vary in size from thousands of acres down to less than one acre, and in general the smaller fisheries have the highest density of fish population. There are good and bad fisheries, but the definition of what is good and what is bad varies between anglers. In a number of cases an angler may describe a fishery as bad because he catches little or nothing there. Another angler who has mastered the techniques required to fish the same water successfully will describe it as excellent. Although it is useful to take notice of other anglers' opinions and to visit those fisheries described as 'excellent', it does not mean that you are guaranteed to catch fish. Successful anglers spend a lot of time researching the water before they manage to catch fish regularly.

The definition of a stillwater fishery has to be vague. A water which relies on natural seepage or springs to maintain water level can honestly be described as a stillwater. However, many fisheries are fed by streams, and it is possible to fish a naturally moving fly. One could describe Loch Tay as a stillwater fishery, certainly stillwater tactics can be used; but it is far from still, and is regularly fished for salmon.

Bayham Abbey is a comparatively small stillwater fishery, but it is fed by a river and drains into the river again at the lower end. The continual water current can be used by the angler to his advantage in presenting dry flies and nymphs at a natural speed which the fish will accept. Concrete bowl reservoirs such as the Queen Mother

Queen Mother Reservoir, Datchet. A concrete bowl reservoir.

Reservoir at Datchet do not have a natural inflow of water, and it has to be pumped into the reservoir. If you can fish near the water intake it can bring spectacular results as this area will often attract fish, especially those feeding on fry.

A stillwater fishery which has been freshly flooded takes some time to settle down. On large reservoirs such as Rutland and Bewl Bridge the filling period will take a number of years. This allows the water to develop naturally, and life forms will be found almost from the time that the fishing opens. The early results from this type of fishery are always very good because fish can feed on food such as worms and beetles which have been caught by the rising water. However, after this initial period of intense feeding on the existing food larder, the fish have to revert to more natural forms of food and the returns of the fishery may show a marked drop before the fish become fully acclimatised. This drop in returns may last for a matter of weeks or for a year or more, depending on the increase of natural food forms in the water, but eventually things will level out. In waters with a high concentration of natural food forms the fish will acclimatise more quickly, and perhaps no drop in returns will be noticed.

Newly dug ponds and gravel pits have no natural life forms, and the fish can find very little food. The growth rate of the fish in this type of water is very slow, and in some cases there is no growth at all. Eventually the water will be colonised by sedges, buzzers, and hopefully fully aquatic life forms upon which the fish can feed. Another fault with this type of water in its early stages is the complete lack of water plant life. Plant life is important to any fishery as this is where the aquatic life forms will live, and the trout will hunt for them there. The trout will also use water plants as cover against detection, and in order to shelter from bright sunlight. Indiscriminate wading in stillwater fisheries reduces or even kills plant life and the food forms in it. This eventually makes the lake margins barren and the fishing consequently harder. Wading should be an option only to be used when necessary. It is an important part of the angler's armoury. A few fishery managers do in fact ban wading in order to preserve the marginal water life.

One other major factor dictates the amount of natural life found in the water, and subsequently the excellence or otherwise of the fish to be caught. That factor is the quality of the water itself.

Although trout can tolerate a certain amount of pollution, any impurity can affect the growth of plant life or food forms. It is therefore necessary that pollution be kept to a minimum. The most recent problem facing fishery owners is the increase in the amounts of nitrates deposited in the water through drainage of fertilised farm land. This can lead to a bloom of algae and bacteria which will reduce the oxygen content of the water dramatically.

Depth of water plays a large part in determining the oxygen content. Small, deep lakes can suffer from lack of oxygen as the water is not turned over frequently enough by the wind. Light cannot penetrate deep water sufficiently to maintain the plant life which is a prime requisite of the trout's main sources of food.

Prime water sources such as streams can provide good clear oxygenated water whereas a fishery depending upon a very slow feeder or seepage may well have problems in the summer when the water warms up.

Acidity does not appear to worry trout too greatly, provided that the levels are kept within reason. The acidity of the water is measured in values of pH, the neutral value being 7 pH. Excess acidity however will affect other life forms including plant life. The still waters of the south-east which are based on or near chalk often show a markedly improved plant life over the still waters of Wales and the south-west which are based on granite, and whose water often drains from acidic peat marshes.

There have been cases of fish kills caused by acidity. The South West Water Authority have experienced this problem at Fernworthy Reservoir on Dartmoor. The over-acidity of the water in the spring killed the rainbow trout in the cages which were anchored in the reservoir. However, over-wintering fish which managed to

Watercress Farm,
Chudleigh, Devon.
A small artificial lake.

congregate around or swim up the less acidic feeder streams survived.

Oxygen is the one thing that all living organisms require. The amount of oxygen in the water is governed by several factors.

The temperature of the water governs the amount of oxygen it contains, and also the efficiency of the trout's respiratory system. Cold water holds a lot of oxygen, and life for the trout is easy. However, when the temperature rises, the oxygen content drops. Coupled with this is the fact that the trout's respiratory system works more efficiently at temperatures below 10 degrees Centigrade. The trout, being cold blooded, lives at the same temperature as the water it is in. Therefore, shallow lakes can become virtual death chambers to trout during a long hot summer.

Plant growth is important to both the trout and its food forms. During bright sunlight plants absorb carbon dioxide and emit oxygen which improves the quality of the water. However, during the night or on dull days the plants will reverse the process and deplete the oxygen content of the water. It is therefore necessary to balance the amount of plant life in order to provide shelter for both trout and food items without the possibility of depleting the oxygen supply too seriously during poor weather conditions. The angler must also be taken into account here, as to continually hook up on weed or, worse still, to continually lose fish in weed will ensure that he will not return.

The disturbance of the water surface by wind and rain also helps to oxygenate the water. A long period of calm warm weather often results in catch returns dropping. A good steady breeze and a few showers of rain will eventually put matters right and get the fish feeding again.

Small waters are often subject to de-oxygenation by the actions of bacteria breaking down leaves and other detritus deposited on the bed of the lake. This again will cause a more serious effect during a warm summer when oxygen levels are already low, with the bacteria being more active and using up more oxygen.

Stillwater trout fisheries have to maintain many different balances in order to be successful:

1. The water must be of good quality.
2. The water must be well oxygenated.
3. The lake must be deep enough to stay reasonably cool, but not too deep as this will result in lack of oxygen and plant life.
4. Plant life must be present to harbour food forms and to produce oxygen, but must not be allowed to thrive to the extent that it could deplete oxygen levels in poor weather conditions, or hamper fishing.

5. The lake must support sufficient food to feed the stock of trout to the extent that they at least maintain their weight and condition.

A fair description of a good stillwater fishery is one that maintains a good head of good quality fish which can grow and thrive in that water. Whether an individual angler can catch them or not is a different matter, but reasonable casting room and good access to the banks are of paramount importance. However, a few trees and bushes around the bank can make the fishing more interesting.

There are many poor stillwater fisheries around at present. If taken to the limit, your local council could put trout in the municipal swimming pool provided that they filled it with pure water. The trout would certainly live, but in a short time their condition would deteriorate. Again, it is possible for a fishery manager to fill his water with double-figure trout and make a name for himself, but sooner or later the standards would drop if the water conditions could not support the stock.

A well-designed and -maintained fishery is a joy to fish. A hole in the ground full of starving, out-of-condition fish is anything but a joy.

Stocking policies vary from water to water. Much depends on the size of the water, and upon the fishing pressure that it is subjected to. Small fisheries can operate a trickle-stocking policy, virtually

Upper Tamar Reservoir. A flooded valley providing natural bank fishing.

replacing numbers of caught fish with new ones on a daily basis. This is the most artificial form of trout fishing. The number and size of the fish are strictly controlled. If few fish are caught, or the management wants some free advertising, the water is overstocked regardless of the volume of natural food available, and the result is a lot of hungry fish which are easily caught. The occasional large fish is put in, and is often caught in a matter of hours, the poor thing not having even got used to its so-called freedom.

With the larger waters there is always a large stocking prior to the start of the season in order to replace fish lost during the winter. The earlier in the year that this initial stocking is carried out, the better. The fish have a chance to distribute themselves throughout the water and to acclimatise themselves to the natural food life. Their scratches, bruises and battered fins can also start to heal. Stocking during the season is always necessary, but the methods can be improved. In order to avoid newly introduced stock fish being caught within hours by the anglers who generally congregate at the stocking points, the new fish should be introduced in small quantities at as many different points as possible. The use of a semi-submersible cage, commonly known as an Irish Boat, which can be towed around the water is probably the best method of all, especially when fish are being transferred from holding cages within the lake. I do not agree that the fish will find their way around if they are all stocked at one point. Rainbow trout shoal very readily, and the introduction of a lot of new fish at one point may easily do more harm than good to the fishing. The mass introduction will almost certainly upset resident stock to the detriment of the fishing, and it may take the water a day or two to settle down. The introduction of a few fish at scattered points around the water causes far less disturbance, and gives an immediate distribution rather than having to wait for days for the stock fish to disperse naturally.

The major talking point of any water is the size of the fish that it contains. All fishery owners stock a few large fish to liven things up occasionally, but it is the average size of stock fish that is the main point of any criticism. There is little point in stocking waters with a few large fish. They are expensive to purchase and stay in the water no longer than smaller fish. At the opposite end of the scale it is equally pointless to stock a water with hundreds of rainbows weighing under a pound. They are easy to catch, and the last thing that we want is boring fishing. My own opinion is that anglers are quite happy with fish of 1¼–1½ lb, provided that they also have a reasonable chance of hooking into something bigger. If the fish average this weight, the angler will be satisfied even if he does not catch his limit. Smaller fish disappoint the angler in general, and almost compel him to fish hard for his limit in order to try to get his money's worth out of the fishery. Fishing is a sport, and the angler wants to enjoy that sport. Most importantly, he is willing to pay for it. The majority of stillwater fisheries are business concerns which must show a profit. The line between profit and loss is very fine, but improved management techniques must benefit both the fishery owners and the angler.

All put-and-take fisheries rely to a great extent on the returns submitted by their anglers to calculate their stocking requirements. It is imperative that returns are submitted, but it is even more imperative that these returns are accurate. Some misguided anglers who catch fish fill in a return stating that they have caught less fish than they actually have in the hope that the fishery management will stock more fish to increase the catch rate. In fact the opposite will happen. If, according to the records, the fish have not been removed, they must still be in the water, therefore fewer new fish will be introduced.

Anglers who take more fish than they are allowed are committing theft. They are taking fish which are the property of the fishery owner. The effect will be the same as with stores suffering from a spate of shoplifting; a price increase to cover pilfering. Everyone suffers.

So please be honest. Fill in your returns accurately, and take only what you are entitled to. If you catch your limit you will have taken about double the rod/day average. You cannot complain about that.

Chapter 3

Your choice of rod

Fishing rods are very personal pieces of equipment. Regardless of how many thousand identical rods may be in use, your rod has its own particular identity – or so it seems.

Personal preferences regarding weight, action, length and power often come before the matter of cost. That is how it should be. Your rod has got to suit you perfectly and also suit the type of fishing to which it is being applied. Today there are so many types of fly rod available that it is possible to leave the tackle shop more confused than when you went in. It is also possible to pay a lot of money for a rod that is not suited to your needs.

Basically a rod must be of a suitable length and power to cast a fly line the distance that you require. It must also be light enough to fish with all day without your getting tired, and sensitive enough to give you enjoyment when fighting a fish.

There is now a multitude of choice of materials, actions, lengths, powers and weights of rod from which the angler can choose, but only a few of these rods are suitable for stillwater trout fishing. One must always bear in mind that quality varies considerably dependent upon the manufacturer. The quality of materials and design is of the utmost importance – to put it bluntly, 'You pay your money and you take your choice.'

Glass fibre

Glass fibre probably made the greatest impact on rod design in the history of angling. The production of a strong yet supple rod made from filaments of glass bonded together with resin signalled the end of the mass-produced cane rods, and to some extent the end of the British rod-manufacturing industry. Cane rods have rightly held their place with river anglers due to their flexibility and easy accurate casting action. However, the excess weight and very high cost has led to them being abandoned by stillwater anglers.

It was not long before we saw glass fibre rods being imported from Eastern Europe and the Far East, and the price dropped very quickly as more manufacturers produced glass fibre pre-impregnated material for rod production. Of course there were and still are good and bad rods. The choice of material and quality of design go hand in hand in determining the action of the rod.

Glass fibre was an improvement over cane for the longer rods because it was lighter and stiffer; it also needed little maintenance. Glass fibre was the first man-made material to be used entirely for the construction of fishing rods. Initially diameters increased, but anglers were prepared to put up with this small inconvenience because of the improvement gained in the areas of weight and action. Gradually, as the trade researched glass fibre the rods improved. Tapers varied, as did wall thicknesses and tube diameters and alternative forms of glass fibre were introduced. Specialist rods were designed for all types of angling.

There is available today a good range of glass-fibre rods which are less expensive than their carbon counterparts. For the angler who wishes to restrict his capital outlay, the occasional angler, or the angler who just wants to see what fly fishing is like, a glass-fibre rod may well be the answer.

Carbon

Carbon was the second breakthrough in rod design. It was developed at the Royal Aircraft Establishment at Farnborough – a thoroughly British achievement. Carbon fibre is lighter and stiffer than glass, therefore less material is required to build a rod. The result was an immediate reduction in weight and diameter. The first carbon blanks to be generally available came from the USA. Thousands of fly rods were produced by many companies on these blanks, and they were expensive. Gradually, however, carbon became more easily available and Japan, Taiwan and Korea began producing rods. In recent years we have seen the price of these rods fall by as much as 50 per cent, a tremendous drop in price in these times of very high inflation. The angler no doubt was pleased to see this reduction as, for many of us, the first carbon rods were out of our price range. However, the question must be asked, 'Just what are we getting for our money?'

Both glass and carbon rods are made by the same basic process. A blank (the tapered tube on which a rod is built) is built on a mandrel which is made, to very accurate tolerances, of either chromed or stainless steel. In most cases the complete blank is built on the mandrel, then cut and spigoted. Push-in or push-over blanks are often made on separate mandrels. The outside diameter of the mandrel equals the internal diameter of the blank.

Firstly the mandrel is completely cleaned, and if necessary it is straightened. Hopefully it will be straight already. If not, you are liable to find that the rod has a bent tip which is one of the most common faults found in any rod. The mandrel is heated in an oven and the pre-preg (the technical term for the carbon or glass cloth) is cut to shape. Pre-preg is supplied in rolls just like curtain material. One edge of the pre-preg is attached to the mandrel with a hot iron. The mandrel, with the pre-preg attached, is then put on a rolling table. The base of the table remains still whilst the top section is lowered onto the mandrel putting it under pressure. The top of the table then moves across almost diagonally, rolling the mandrel across the table base, and the pre-preg rolls around the mandrel. The mandrel, complete with the pre-preg, is now wrapped in cellophane. This ensures that the pre-preg stays in place, and also ensures that the resin which is impregnated into the cloth does not melt out and away from the blank.

The mandrel is then put in a special oven set at a predetermined temperature for a set period of time. During this period the resin will melt and soak completely through the pre-preg, then cool and harden. The mandrel is removed from the oven, and is then pulled out of the blank. The cellophane is removed from the outside of the blank, and the ends of the blank are trimmed.

In many cases the blank is put through a centreless grinder to give it a smooth finish. If this operation is omitted the blank will have a definite spiral to it caused by the wraps of cellophane. Many blanks are now sold unground, and some anglers believe that this is a sign of cheapness or lower quality. This is not necessarily so. One train of thought is that if a blank is ground some of the strength is taken away. This may well be possible; however, when a blank is designed, the designer should decide whether or not it is to be ground, making the necessary allowances at this stage. The financial saving by omitting the grinding would not reduce the cost of the blank significantly anyway.

There are fewer than ten firms producing blanks in the United Kingdom, but numerous companies import blanks from America, Europe and the Far East. The blanks are sold to rod manufacturers and retail shops who either sell them to the DIY angler, or build rods themselves. It is therefore possible to purchase two different rods which are made up on the same blank. Of course the guides and fittings will be different, but the action of the rods will be virtually identical.

Carbon is the most popular of the rod-building materials in use at the moment, and it is the quality and quantity of carbon used in a rod which has caused the tremendous range of prices we see today. It is possible to buy a carbon fly rod for £30. It is also possible to pay £120 for a rod which appears very similar. Why is it that these similar 'carbon' rods should differ so much in price?

Carbon is a man-made fibre. It is in fact rayon which has been burnt in a special furnace under strictly controlled conditions. The rayon filaments, which are much finer than a human hair, pass through the furnace continually, many thousands at a time in ropes called tows. The number of filaments in a tow depends on the thickness of the filaments. Fine filaments are more expensive than thick filaments as the amount of carbon produced per hour is reduced accordingly. The quality of the carbon is reflected by its percentage of purity. Therefore you can have 99.9 per cent pure carbon or 70 per cent pure carbon. Having established this fact it would seem to follow that 99.9 per cent carbon makes 99.9 per cent carbon rods. It does not.

In the vast majority of cases, the carbon filaments come out of the furnace and are passed through combs to spread them out flat. They are then laid on to a scrim of very fine woven fibre glass. The reason for this is that it is impossible to wrap carbon filaments around a mandrel as they have to run along, and not around, the blank. Therefore they are stuck to the glass scrim beforehand. The complete material can then be wrapped around the mandrel with the carbon fibres laid longitudinally along the mandrel, giving the blank the strength it requires when casting or fighting a fish. This does mean, however, that this type of blank has poor resistance to crushing. Therefore, in virtually all carbon rods there is a percentage of glass, which means that although you can have a rod made of

Carbon pre-impregnated material. Notice how the carbon fibres run one way. The woven fibre glass scrim is clearly visible underneath.

99.9 per cent pure carbon, the actual carbon content of the blank is a lot less than that.

Here, we come up against the main problem facing the angler when he goes out to buy a carbon rod. If we forget the resin content of the pre-preg, it is perfectly feasible to use various densities of glass-fibre scrim and carbon to manufacture blanks with varying carbon content. A heavy glass scrim which has a layer of fine carbon fibres laid along it will look like a carbon blank because the carbon will show on the outside of the blank. However, analysis will show a low carbon content. A light glass scrim with a layer of dense carbon fibres will be analysed as a high carbon content blank, but it will not look any different.

As the price war hotted up, blank manufacturers developed the use of carbon fibre even further. Blanks can now be produced with a carbon-glass-carbon sandwich effect. It is also possible to put a wrap of carbon around the outside of a glass blank. No doubt, both these methods of manufacture improve what would otherwise be an ordinary glass blank, but although the rods will have a carbon content they cannot be described as carbon rods. They are in fact carbon/glass composites.

In general, a good carbon rod will have a mix of approximately 86 per cent carbon to 14 per cent glass measured by weight and excluding the resin content which has to be there to hold the blank together. On the other hand carbon content can be as low as 15 per cent.

Quality and quantity of carbon are therefore major factors affecting the price of rods. There is however another important factor which is just as likely to affect performance of rods.

Research and development is the key to producing top quality rods. It is possible for a rod manufacturer to go to Japan, Taiwan or Korea and buy blanks off the peg. These blanks are sold all around the world. They are a mixture of ideas from around the globe, and are best described as general purpose blanks. Many British companies use these blanks to produce inexpensive and mid-price-range rods.

The difference comes when you set about designing a rod for a specific purpose. It is not uncommon to test a dozen prototypes made of various types of carbon on different mandrels. An experienced angler can give an immediate assessment of what is required to improve a blank. That is the easy part. It is the experience of the development engineer and his workforce that determines whether that blank can be improved or not. It may well be that on occasions the impossible is asked, but what may be impossible to one engineer might be basic develoment to a more experienced man.

The thorough and expert research by top men in their field is very expensive, but in the long run the ultimate product will be of better quality but consequently higher priced.

In recent years there has been a lot of discussion about high- and low-modulus carbon. Modulus is the technical term for stiffness. The stiffer a material, the higher its modulus, but the higher the modulus of a material the more brittle it becomes. Standard carbon has a modulus of about 33 million pounds per square inch, which is approximately the same as steel. High-modulus carbon has a modulus of 50 million psi. It is very much stiffer, but more brittle. If you compare steel and cast iron you will understand the principle more readily. Cast iron is stiffer than steel and is therefore of a higher modulus, but cast iron is brittle because it is so stiff. Steel bends under stress, but cast iron breaks.

The same rule applies to high-modulus carbon. It is stiffer, and can therefore be used to make lighter, slimmer rods. It is however more susceptible to damage through knocks by being dropped, and also by overstress caused by bad casting techniques and abuse. A badly timed cast or an attempt to lift too much line from the water can result in high-modulus carbon breaking. High- and low-modulus carbon can be mixed on the same blank to give stiffness where it is required without increasing weight or diameter.

There is still a lot of research and development going on with carbon. It is a most versatile material, and will be with us for many

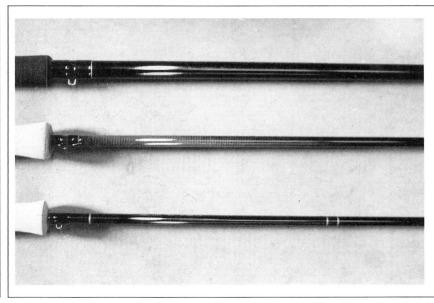

Three rods of identical length and line rating show the difference in diameter of: *(Top)* Fibre Glass, *(Centre)* Carbon Fibre, *(Bottom)* Boron.

years to come. Boron is the latest material to become involved in blank construction. It no doubt has its uses, but also has its drawbacks. Boron is made by fusing tungsten filaments. Tungsten is a metal, and is therefore very stiff and heavy. There is no such thing as a 100 per cent boron rod – it is a physical impossibility. Boron can help in blank construction by stiffening sections that require it, without increasing the diameter of the section. Boron composite rods are slimmer than carbon rods, and if the development is carried out properly they will have a crisper action which can help improve casting distance. They are however expensive. Boron is used in conjunction with carbon to reduce rod diameter and to improve the action, but it can never be used on its own.

To sum up, in general a carbon rod is probably the best buy. Having said that, there are a number of good fibre-glass rods available that have a better action than some of the less expensive carbon rods, although they might be slightly heavier and greater in diameter than the latter. As far as carbon rods are concerned it is better to pay more and purchase a rod which has been designed specifically for stillwater trout fishing. Boron rods are expensive, but they can help increase casting distance because of their crisper action. However, here again it is better to buy a more expensive boron rod in order to ensure that it has been designed properly.

Having dealt with blanks, it is necessary to take a look at the guides and fittings that go to make up the rod. *Rod rings* have developed

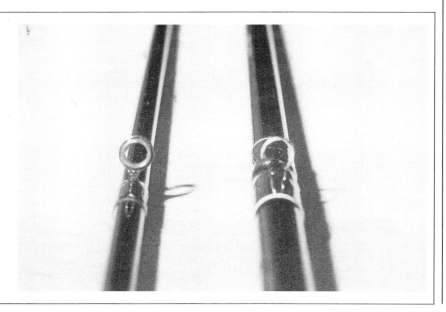

(Left) A Fuji single leg guide which keeps the fly line away from the blank. *(Right)* A snake ring which keeps the fly line very close to the blank.

significantly during the last few years. Hard chrome snake rings are popular on cane rods, and are often fitted to less expensive carbon and glass rods. Some anglers maintain that snake rings offer less resistance to the line during casting, but it is also possible that these rings keep the line too close to the blank causing it to drag on the blank and so reduce casting distance. Snake rings are very light and flexible. They are suitable for shorter rods where presentation rather than distance is important. Avoid plain wire or metal guides. These tend to be rather heavy and are stiff which can alter the action of the blank. They are also susceptible to wear; a worn ring can ruin the surface of a fly line, and cut through monofilament in record time.

The most popular *guides* are now the aluminium-oxide guides developed by Fuji. The butt guide, which has to be sturdy, is usually the model BNHG–B, and the single-leg intermediate guides are the model BFG. The Fuji guides are both strong and light, being pressed from a single piece of steel — no joints to break or corrode. The aluminium-oxide centres are virtually wear proof and are highly polished in order to keep friction to a minimum. This aids casting distance and reduces wear on the fly line.

The ultimate in guides must be the new Fuji SIC range. Silicon carbide replaces the aluminium oxide centres. It is much lighter and harder, and it also dissipates heat much faster than any other material which helps protect the nylon leader against melting if you are fighting a large fish on a long leader. Silicon carbide is so hard

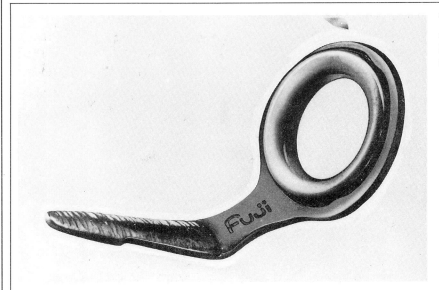

The Fuji SG guide. A silicon carbide single leg guide specifically for fly rods.

that it will resist attempts to groove it with a file. The SIC guides are more expensive than standard guides, but will certainly help to increase casting distance. The overall weight of the rod will be reduced, and they will not impair the action of the blank. The main advantage, of course, is that they will never need to be replaced.

The shape of the *rod handle* is important as it must be of a suitable size and shape to fit your hand comfortably. Cork is the favourite material as it is light and does not absorb water. Many rods are now sold with shrink tube covering the handle to keep it clean. This should be removed before the rod is used as it becomes slippery when wet, and does not have the slight 'give' that makes cork so suitable. The quality of a cork handle can be ascertained by the amount of filler used to plug the natural holes in the cork. Top-quality cork needs little filler, but the poorer quality cork has numerous flaws which need to be filled before the handle is given its final sanding.

Recently, more rods have been fitted with EVA handles. EVA is a material like a sponge rubber, but the cells are very small, making the material dense and waterproof. A good EVA handle, probably made of Orblon or Hypalon, should have the same basic feel to it as cork. In wet weather it can offer a better grip than cork, and feels warmer.

The most common shape of handle is the double fishtail. This shape is almost universal on any rod over 9 feet as it offers a better

(Above) A metal screw-lock fitting combined with an EVA handle. *(Below)* A Fuji FPS fitting combined with a high quality cork handle.

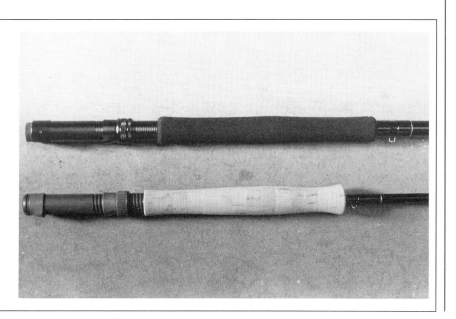

grip and a flared front end to rest the thumb on. The cigar-shaped handle is best suited to shorter rods of up to 8 feet. Rods of this length are not used for distance casting, and the cigar shape is very comfortable.

Be sure to check that the handle of the rod fits snugly into your hand. There is nothing worse than a handle that rubs against your thumb or is too small or too large to offer a good positive grip.

Reel fittings vary considerably in design and efficiency. The main objective is to hold the reel securely in place. The screw lock fitting is the most popular, and is available in a range of sizes to fit all rods. The Fuji FPS, a carbon-reinforced nylon fitting, is both light and secure. Metal variations are available if you prefer. Avoid fittings incorporating sliding rings on longer rods as the reel can work loose.

There has been a great deal of discussion regarding which way up a screw lock fitting should be fitted on to a rod. It is really a matter of choice. Many anglers prefer the reel to be fitted at the butt of the rod to help balance, and to keep the reel away from the hand. Other anglers prefer the reel set an inch or two up the butt so that the reel is protected should the rod butt be dropped on the ground. The placing of the reel certainly makes a difference to the feel of the rod when casting, but it is a matter for the individual angler to choose exactly what he wants.

There is then a large variation in rod design, and the angler

Fuji FPS fittings specially designed for fly rods.

should be able to find a rod fitted with the accessories that he requires without having to either build a rod himself, or have one custom built for him.

Having dealt with rod building materials and accessories, it is of the utmost importance to decide on the physical requirements of your rod. *Length, power* and *action* are the three major factors which ultimately decide which rod is suitable for the situation the angler finds himself in.

The length of the rod governs to some extent the distance that it is capable of casting. Obviously a proficient caster will do better than a novice using the same rod, but it is possible to handicap yourself by using a rod that is either too long or too short. A longer rod will help you to keep your fly line above ground obstructions on the back cast, but if you are fishing under trees a rod which is too long will obviously cause problems. The longer the rod, the more tiring it can be to use; therefore the angler must initially select a length of rod suitable for the fisheries he intends to fish, and one which he can use all day without becoming too tired. On smaller waters where distance casting is not required an 8½ foot rod may well be ideal. On larger waters a 9½ foot or even 10 foot rod may well be more suitable. A longer rod helps the angler to hook fish at distance as it picks the line up more quickly. There is a limit however. For bank fishing a 10½ foot rod is probably the maximum length suitable. Longer rods are available, but they are really designed for boat fishing where continuous long distance casting is not required.

There are many variations to boat fishing, some of them very specialist, and numerous rods can be considered suitable. However, a rod of 9½ feet is probably the shortest that will allow the angler to fish effectively. Rods of 10 and 10½ feet are more suitable for general boat fishing, and if you intend to fish loch style, an 11 or even 12 foot rod will serve you well.

Unless you intend to specialise it is best to select the longest rod that will suit your fishing in general. Bear in mind the type of fishery that you intend to visit, and decide whether you will spend more time on the bank or in a boat. Take into account bank space, the size of the fishery, and the distances that you are likely to have to cast. The action of the rod dictates the casting distance, the capability of controlling fish, and to some extent the breaking strain of the leader that you will be able to use. Basically there are three types of action, but today with the number of rods and their differing actions it is sometimes difficult to identify a specific action.

The through action (sometimes called soft action) is not very popular with stillwater anglers. Blanks with a slow taper usually have a through action which means that when a rod is under pressure it bends right through to the butt. This type of rod is more popular with anglers who fish downstream wet fly where short casting is the norm, and the take of a fish is registered on the rod tip. The soft, forgiving action of this rod means that light leaders can be used as the rod cushions the plunges of the fish, acting like a shock absorber. However, the through action does not help distance casting as quite a large percentage of the power put into the cast by the angler is lost before it reaches the tip of the rod, which actually works the line. A large fish can prove difficult to control on a through-action rod due to the lack of power in the butt section.

The middle-to-tip action is without doubt the most popular action. There is enough power in the butt of the rod to enable the angler to cast a good distance, and this power also helps to pick up a fair amount of line off the water and hook fish at a distance. Controlling a fish on a rod with some power in the butt is much easier than with a soft rod. The casting action is slightly faster and certainly crisper than that of a through-action rod. The middle-to-tip action rod is the ideal model to start with. It will effectively cast all types of line including shooting heads, but besides casting well it is good to fish with. Due to its popularity, the majority of rods are of this design but it must be said that some are better than others.

The tip-action rod in its ultimate form can be classed as a

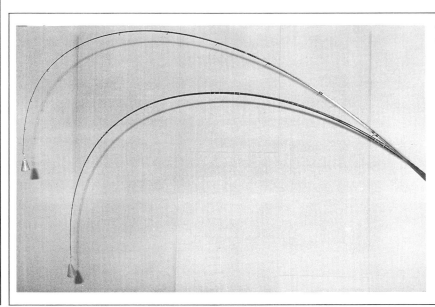

Two rods of the same length and AFTM rating show the difference between a tip action and a middle action.

specialist rod. It is designed primarily to cast distances with either weight forward or shooting head lines. Tournament casters will use a rod with a tip action as the rod will transmit the caster's power efficiently to the tip section where that power is transferred into line speed and subsequently into casting distance. The Speed Tip fly rod developed by Normark has a spliced tip which helps create a very narrow casting loop. The rest of the blank is very stiff to transmit power to the tip. It is designed for shooting heads and is highly specialised. Leader strengths have to be increased with this type of rod because they can transmit so much power that ordinary leaders may well be in danger of breaking. All in all, the tip-action rod, whilst being very useful, is not a beginner's rod but something that may be added to your armoury later in order to deal with a specific aspect of your fishing.

The remaining item, which is of utmost importance when selecting a rod, is that of *line rating*. On each rod you will find either the letters AFTM or the sign # followed by two or three figures such as 7–8 or 6–7–8. These figures are given as a guide by the rod manufacturer as to which lines are suitable for that rod. All fly lines are rated according to their weight, a matter which we shall cover later in this book, and the rod manufacturers therefore rate their rods in the same way. The only problem is that whilst lines can be accurately rated, the manufacturer will rate his rods according to his

Three rods of identical length and action show the difference in power required for AFTM 5–6 – AFTM 7–8 – AFTM 9–10.

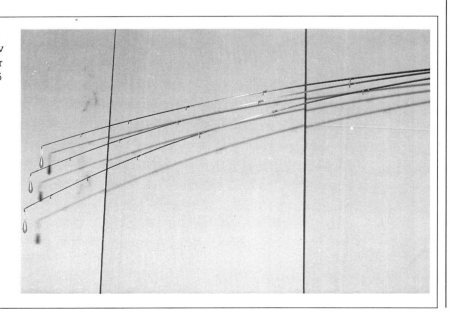

own experience. Therefore it is possible to have a rod rated as 6–7 which may either cast a size 5 line or a size 8 line better than the lines that it has been designed for. This of course also depends a lot upon your own casting skills.

The AFTM ratings suitable for stillwater fishing run from AFTM 4 at the light end to AFTM 9 at the heavy end. Anglers fishing the general type of stillwater fisheries usually prefer a rod rating of between 6 and 8 in conjunction with a 9½ foot to 10 foot rod. On smaller fisheries where shorter rods are used and distance casting is not required, an AFTM 4–5 will suffice. The angler must bear in mind that a heavier line will in general cast further, and will penetrate a head-on wind better than a light line, but it will also make more disturbance when it hits the water.

There is very little point in using a rod of 8 feet rated AFTM 8–9 in the hope of casting a good distance. The length of the rod itself will restrict you. At the other end of the scale a 10½ foot rod rated at AFTM 4–5 will be very light and supple. Whilst it may cast well in good weather, as soon as you are faced with a head wind your line will have no penetration. Having said that, an 11 foot rod rated at AFTM 5–6 will be superb for loch-style fishing which does not require long-distance casting, and where all casting is done either down or cross wind.

For general stillwater fishing therefore, the angler has to settle for a rod that is capable of functioning adequately for two or three different types of fishing. Whilst a rod rated 7–8 may be heavy for loch-style fishing, it will be suitable for general bank fishing or for fishing from an anchored boat. In general terms, the shorter the rod, the lighter the line rating, but AFTM 9 is just about the limit. Once a rod over 10½ feet is employed, the line rating should again reduce as the outfit will prove to be too heavy to cast all day singlehanded. The longer the rod the more leverage it has, and this will affect your wrist considerably.

As a guide, the following combinations should prove acceptable, but it is the angler who must make the final decision.

Situation	Length	Action	AFTM	
Small lake	8½'	Through	5–6	
Small–medium lake	9'	Mid-tip	6–7	
Medium–large lake	9½'	Mid-tip	7–8*	
Medium–large lake	10'	Mid-tip	7–8*	
Large exposed water	10'	Mid-tip	8–9*	*These rods are also
Loch style	10½'	Through	5–6	suitable for fishing
Loch style	11'	Through	6–7	from an anchored
Loch style	11½'	Through	6–7	boat.

Bear in mind that actions, ratings, and the weight of the rod vary from manufacturer to manufacturer, and it is worth trying a few rods before making a final decision.

Chapter 4

Your choice of lines

If ever there was a subject guaranteed to spark off heated discussion or even argument, this is it. Just what do you look for in a fly line? What is the difference between a line costing £8 and a line costing £30? Is a double taper better than a weight forward? And so the questions go on, and the answers are often a matter of a particular angler's preference. All anglers have their own preferences which are based on their style of fishing and the type of water that they fish. Their choice of branded lines are based on cost, quality, suitability, and more often than not the fact that they have used the same make for years.

Luckily for us, fly-line manufacture has improved a lot over the last few years. No longer do we have to use silk lines that must be treated in order to float, which by the end of the day have become slow sinkers and then have to be dried and re-treated. Mind you, silk lines are still made, and a surprisingly large number of trout anglers use them for river fishing. Good luck to them, but silk lines are not a serious proposition for stillwater fly fishing.

The fly lines of today are usually based on a braided core, often of Terylene. The plastic coating is applied by machine geared to very accurate tolerances, and it is the distribution of this plastic coat which dictates the AFTM rating, and the type of line that is produced. Low-density plastic is used for floating lines, higher-density plastic is used for sinking lines – the higher the density of the plastic, the faster the line will sink. Basically, most lines can be produced on one grade of braided core. However, at least one manufacturer of top quality lines uses a different grade of braid for each AFTM rating of line.

The type of plastic used will also dictate how supple or stiff a line will be, and also how smooth the finish. Very supple lines, while nice to handle, will not shoot as well through the guides as they sag and create friction. A line that is too stiff may shoot very well, but will be very difficult to handle on a figure-of-eight retrieve. The finish of a fly line must be as smooth as possible in order to reduce drag, and to be comfortable to handle. It must also stand up to a great deal of wear and tear.

Sinking lines are usually produced in shades of green and brown. Visibility from the angler's point of view is not so very necessary, but browns and greens tend to blend in well with the fish's surroundings. Cortland however produce a blue Intermediate line, their reason being that the trout are looking up towards the line which will then blend in with the sky.

The colour of floating lines however is a different matter. White, cream, yellow, green, peach, red and grey are all available. Many anglers swear by greys and greens which they feel are less visible to the fish. I am not so sure. Not so many years ago I was involved in scuba diving and, from my experience, a line on the top of the water showed up as silver. It may be that the surface of the water is reflected down from under the fly line. It was certainly difficult to distinguish colour unless the water was flat calm. I therefore do not think that the colour of a floating line matters very much as far as the fish are concerned. Having said that, there is a possibility that very light coloured lines may flash during casting and put the fish down.

The important point about floating-line colour is that the angler must be able to see the line well enough to detect the takes of a trout. White lines would seem to be the obvious choice, but if the water is reflecting a silver colour white is very difficult to see. Water usually reflects silver, grey, blue or black, therefore these colours should be avoided. Peach, red, light green and yellow would therefore appear to be the colours to seriously consider when buying a floating line.

When selecting a fly line it is therefore necessary to check that:
The plastic coating is of a reasonable thickness, otherwise it will crack.
The plastic coating is not so thick that it will stiffen the line to the extent that it becomes difficult to handle.
The finish is smooth and free from blemishes.
The line is of a suitable colour.

Floating lines

As mentioned previously, the density of the plastic coating dictates whether a line floats or sinks. The density of the plastic on a floating line is very low. In fact, the lower the better, because the line will ride higher in the surface film, and will be easier to lift off. (No line actually floats on the surface film of the water, they all float in it to a greater or lesser degree.) The plastic coating is full of air bubbles to help the line float. Floatant can be applied to increase the line's buoyancy, and this is often needed at the tip of the line which will often be seen to sink slightly.

The floating line is probably the most adaptable line available to the stillwater angler. It will present dry flies, wet flies, nymphs (leaded or unleaded) and lures. Depending upon the length of the leader it can be used to present flies down to about 5 feet using a slow retrieve. Greater depth can be achieved by using a leaded fly in conjunction with a long leader and waiting for the fly to sink. The floating line is therefore the most important line that the angler has in his possession.

The angler has three choices regarding the type of floating line that he buys.

Double taper

The most adaptable type of line, the double taper (DT) aerialises well and gives excellent presentation. It does not shoot as well as a weight forward or shooting head, but distance can be achieved by aerialising more line. The DT can also be lifted off the water more easily than other lines, and a change of direction of up to 90 degrees can be achieved by using only one false cast. This is extremely useful when fishing a rise where accurate casts need to be made quickly to fish that have been seen.

Weight forward

Designed for achieving distance without the necessity of using lots of false casts. The weight forward (WF) does not present the fly with such delicacy as the DT due to its uneven distribution of

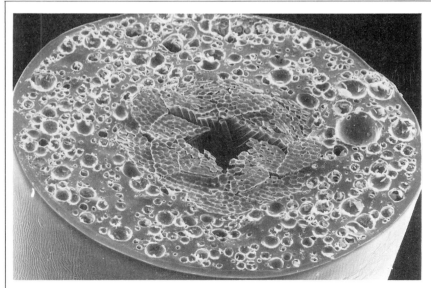

An electron microphoto of a floating Cortland fly line. There are three parts to a fly line: the braided core, the plastic covering and the smooth outer casing. In the case of a floating line the plastic covering is full of air bubbles. *(Photo: Cortland Line Co. USA)*

Fly line profiles.
(Top) Double taper.
(Centre) Standard
weight forward.
(Bottom) Standard 30'
shooting head.

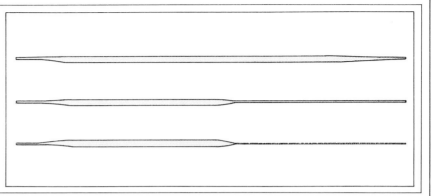

weight. It is not so easily controlled as the DT line, the weight-forward section having to be retrieved into the rod rings before lifting the line off the water. Nor can a change of direction be made so easily.

Shooting head

Designed purely for distance, the shooting head (ST) offers poor presentation of the fly. Due to its construction, the angler cannot vary the amount of line that he wishes to aerialise. On no account can the ST line be lifted off the water and cast into another direction. The ST line is therefore not really suitable for either dry fly or nymph fishing. Should it be used for long-range wet fly or nymph fishing it is highly likely that offers by trout at such range would prove very difficult to detect, and even more difficult to hook.

Sinking lines

The most important factor to bear in mind regarding sinking lines is the rate at which they will sink. It is no good having a line that sinks so slowly that you have to wait for ages for it to reach the correct depth. Conversely, it is no good having a line that sinks so quickly that your fly ends up below the fish where it will not be seen. It follows therefore that the angler will usually have more than one sinking line in order to be able to fish effectively all the time.

Intermediate or neutral density

The slowest of all the sinking lines is the Intermediate or Neutral Density line. This is most commonly used for fishing sub-surface nymphs, wet flies or lures when the fish are taking just under the surface. It is an ideal line for fishing nymphs in a cross wind where the belly caused in a floating line will be avoided. Either double-taper or weight-forward versions are suitable, depending upon the angler's requirements, but it has been found that a few of the double-taper lines tend to sink more quickly in the middle than they do at either end, causing a large belly of line under the water, and a slower indication of takes. The Intermediate line is equally useful from either bank or boat, and has proved to be very useful in loch-style fishing.

Slow sinker

A favourite line of many anglers, this is suitable for nymphs, wet flies and lures. It is ideal for fishing shallow waters as it will help avoid the fly hooking up on the bottom. However, when fishing deeper waters it may sink too slowly and waste a lot of fishing time. Both double-taper and weight-forward models are suitable, but as presentation may not be quite so important, the weight-forward line is often favoured.

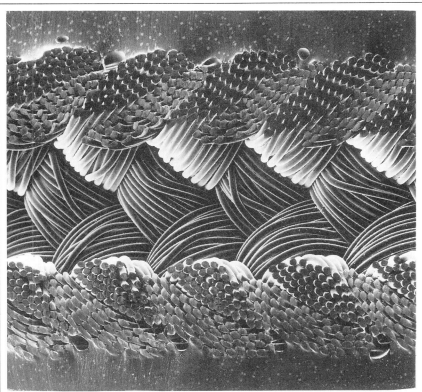

A longitudinal cross section of a Cortland sinking line. The braided core is clearly seen together with the coating. The flecks in the coating are the sinking compound which control the density of the line. (*Photo: Cortland Line Co. USA*)

Sinking rates. The density of the line controls the sink rate. This graph shows the sinking rate of Cortland fly lines. *(Cortland Line Co. USA)*

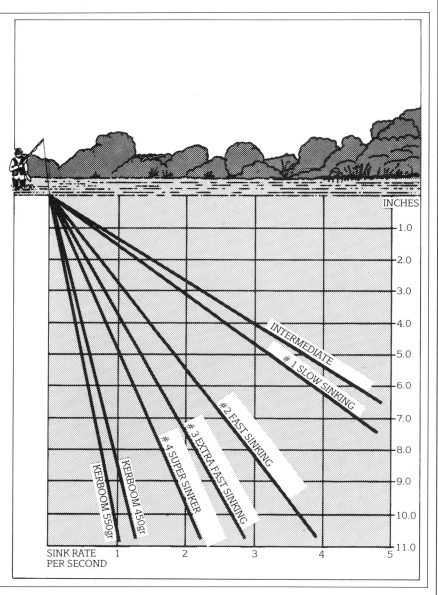

INCHES

1.0
2.0
3.0
4.0
5.0
6.0
7.0
8.0
9.0
10.0
11.0

INTERMEDIATE
#1 SLOW SINKING
#2 FAST SINKING
#3 EXTRA FAST SINKING
#4 SUPER SINKER
KERBOOM 450gr
KERBOOM 550gr

SINK RATE PER SECOND   1   2   3   4   5

Standard sinker

This is without doubt the most popular sinking line. It is suitable for wet flies and lures, but is rarely used for nymph fishing. Due to the depth at which the flies are fished, presentation is even less important, and weight-forward or shooting-head lines are favourite. The Standard Sinker can be used equally well from both bank and boat, and is often useful for loch-style fishing when the fish are feeding deeper in the water.

Really a line for deep fishing, this can be used from the bank, but **Fast sinker**
the speed of retrieve may have to be increased in order to prevent
the lure snagging on the bottom. Unless the line is used for loch-
style fishing there is little point in using a double-taper line. Without
a doubt, distance is a necessity when using a Fast Sinker, and a
weight-forward or shooting-head line is the answer.

This line is usually lead impregnated. As its name suggests, it sinks **Extra fast sinker**
very quickly. Here again, presentation is not very important, and
therefore weight-forward or shooting-head lines are favoured in
order to achieve distance. The Extra Fast Sinker is almost always
used from a boat unless of course the bank angler is fishing into
very deep water. This type of line is favoured for deep fishing with
large lures on waters such as Grafham and Rutland. It does not
have a regular place on small put-and-take fisheries where the
splash of it hitting the water could frighten every fish within casting
distance.

The Lead Core line is exactly what its name suggests. It is comprised **Lead core**
of a plastic coating or a braid over a core of lead. This line can only
be used in the form of either a shooting head or a trolling line. It is
strictly a lure fisherman's line, designed for fishing anything up to
40 feet deep. It is very heavy, and highly uncontrollable in the air.
The Lead Core is an expert's line only, and certainly not a line to
learn on.

So far, I have not mentioned the shooting head in any detail. This **Shooting head**
relatively new development in fly fishing seems to have taken hold
lately to the extent that some newcomers to the sport can do little
more than cast a shooting head. They are missing a great deal of
enjoyment. The shooting head lacks delicacy of presentation, the
ability to change casting direction when the line is extended, and
limits the angler to aerialising the length of the head only.
    Due to the shooting head's limitations it is doubtful that a floating
shooting head is of much use. The poor presentation is the most
significant factor, but to be perfectly truthful, I find it hard enough to
detect takes on the nymph at 25 yards. I certainly would not stand
much chance at 40 yards. The inability to either lift off the water, or

to recast in a different direction, limits the use of a shooting head during a rise, and it is not versatile enough to cope with the many situations that we encounter during a season's fishing. I am not sure that I am personally in favour of shooting heads for intermediate lines for exactly the same reasons as I dislike them for floating lines.

There is no doubt however that shooting heads have helped anglers increase their catches on sinking lines. The shooting head, used properly, will certainly increase the average angler's casting distance, and when used in conjunction with either wet flies or lures on a medium-speed retrieve or faster will increase catches due to the fact that the angler will cover more fish; the angler will be relying on feeling the take of the fish rather than seeing it. Trout usually take flies retrieved slowly very gently, and have time to eject it before the angler is aware that anything is happening. On medium and fast retrieves the fish has more chance of being hooked immediately it takes the fly rather than when the angler waits to see the take and then reacts.

Extra fast sinkers and lead core lines are ideal for shooting heads. When fishing deep from a boat, distance is essential in order to attain maximum depth and still have a reasonably long horizontal retrieve. The fine running line creates less resistance and allows the head to sink almost vertically rather than swinging in towards the boat. The reduction in resistance also reduces the pressure on the leader when fighting a fish.

Sink tip

The one line that remains to be mentioned is the Sink Tip (F/S). Here again the name is descriptive. In general a 10 foot section of sinking line is joined to a floating line. The tip will sink and present the fly under the surface whilst the rest of the line stays on the surface to hold up the sinking portion. In practice it will be found necessary to apply lots of floatant to the floating section of line, otherwise it will slowly sink. The sink tip will therefore allow the angler to present the fly deeper than on a floating line, whilst still having some of the advantages that a floating line offers with regard to bite detection.

The only problem with a sink-tip line is that due to the different densities of line it is not easy to cast. It is difficult to obtain the usually smooth turnover that can be expected with ordinary floating or sinking lines. This is due to the fact that the sinking section is heavier than the rest of the line, and tends to collapse on to the water. A short, sharp pull on the line as it turns over on the forward cast may well solve the problem, but casting distance is reduced. Many anglers have turned to the Intermediate line in recent years.

The choice of line is therefore almost limitless. There are literally hundreds to choose from. The most sound advice is to buy the best line that you can afford, and then look after it.

Chapter 5

Matching rods and lines

One of the most commonly asked questions of any fishing tackle dealer regarding fly fishing tackle is 'What line do I need for this rod?' Very rarely are we asked, 'What rod will suit this line?' You may think this a ridiculous comment, but in fly fishing the rod and line work more closely together than in any other form of fishing. In sea fishing, coarse fishing and other forms of game fishing where spinners or bait are used, an artificial weight is tied on to or near the end of the line. This weight helps the angler to cast. In fly fishing there is no added weight. The actual fly line is the weight, and this must suit the rod perfectly in order to ensure good casting.

Some years ago the American Fishing Tackle Manufacturers Association agreed on a formula to ratify fly line weights. This is the well-known AFTM number (already discussed in Chapter 3) which you will find printed on both rods and lines. It is recognised all over the world, and is probably the only truly recognised formula ever to be accepted by the angling trade.

The AFTMA fly line standards

Code	Minimum weight	Maximum weight
1	54 grains	66 grains
2	74 grains	86 grains
3	94 grains	106 grains
4	114 grains	126 grains
5	134 grains	146 grains
6	152 grains	168 grains
7	177 grains	193 grains
8	202 grains	218 grains
9	230 grains	250 grains
10	270 grains	290 grains
11	318 grains	342 grains
12	368 grains	392 grains

You will often see rods rated AFTM 6–7 or 7–8. This means that the rod is best suited to aerialising 30 feet of either a 6 or 7 line, or a 7 or 8 line respectively.

The AFTMA agreed to weigh the first 30 feet of fly line (excluding the final tapered tip section) and depending upon the number of grains it weighed, an AFTM number was allocated to the line according to the table that they had drawn up. It mattered not whether the line was double taper, weight forward, floating, or fast sinking. It was the weight of the line that was measured – nothing else. A sinking line is no heavier than a floating line of the same rating – it just has a higher density. This is one of the most important points to bear in mind when selecting either fly lines or rods. The AFTM number printed on a rod means that it is most suitable for aerialising 30 feet (10 yards) of a similarly rated fly line.

That thirty feet is a very important figure. A rod manufacturer is telling you that his rod is designed for aerialising 30 feet of a specifically rated fly line. The standard weight-forward lines have a 30 foot weight-forward section. This is no coincidence. They are designed that way in order that the angler does not aerialise too much fly line. Many weight-forward lines are returned to manufacturers under complaint when signs of cracking appear in the coating of the running line just behind the weight-forward section. This is no fault of the line. It is due to the fact that the angler has been aerialising too much line, and the wear from the tip guide has been imparted to the running line which is not designed to take that sort of punishment. It follows therefore that we should restrict ourselves to aerialising only 30 feet of fly line. No more and no less.

Now I am the first to admit that this is impossible. We may not need to aerialise as much as 30 feet, or we may want to aerialise more depending upon the situation. So we must reach a compromise. Let us consider the individual parts played by both the rod and the line during the cast.

Any fly rod when not under strain is straight. If yours is not, then it is time to invest in a new one. Pressure must be exerted on the rod to bend it, but the rod, when under strain, will exert its own pressure in an attempt to return to the straight position. The rod is therefore a spring. Remember the old school trick of flicking a piece of blotting paper soaked in ink with your ruler, a painful memory for some. The ruler was the spring, forcing the blotting paper forward when it returned to its normal position. A fly rod does exactly the same job – it propels the line forward.

The act of lifting the rod compresses it, and as it springs back it shoots the line out behind you. The act of pushing the rod forward compresses it again, and it throws the fly line forward as it straightens. The single and double hauls increase the compression of the rod, thereby making it exert more pressure on the line as it recovers its straight position, increasing the line speed which in turn increases distance. A fly rod, however, cannot be held under compression with a finger like our school ruler; there must be a weight applied to the rod in order to make it compress. This is the reason why the fly line is so important. It is the fly line that acts as the weight to compress the rod.

Let us go back to the school ruler again. If only a light pressure was applied, your blotting paper would not go anywhere. It would just fall off the end of the ruler. In the extreme, if too much pressure was applied the ruler would break. Somewhere in between the two extremes there was a position where exactly the right pressure was applied to send the blotting paper sailing the length of the classroom to hit the teacher on the back of the neck.

The same reasoning applies to your rod and line. There is an ideal point where the rod and line match each other exactly, and provided that your casting technique is up to scratch, this is the point which will result in a cast of optimum distance. If the line is too light you cannot compress the rod sufficiently for it to throw the line forward. If the line is too heavy, the rod will be incapable of exerting enough pressure against the weight of the line, and the line will collapse on the ground behind you.

Let us take as an example an angler who fishes medium-sized reservoirs, and likes a 9½ foot rod because it suits his casting style and the types of fisheries that he visits. He cannot use a light line (AFTM 4–5) because on occasions he has to cast into the wind, and for that reason he needs a line with some weight to penetrate. On the other hand he does not want to fish a heavy line (AFTM 9–10) because it may well disturb fish when he is fishing close in.

Our angler therefore goes for the old favourite reservoir rod, a 9½ foot AFTM 7–8. Fine. He cannot go far wrong with this rod although he may decide to specialise later and buy other rods for specific purposes.

The question now arises as to which line he should buy. We must discount the fact that he will need both a floater and a sinker, that is obvious. But which type of line will suit him best? Personal preference plays a large part here. He may prefer weight forward or he may prefer double taper. He may even decide to go for a shooting head. The matter is entirely up to him.

The real problem arises when our angler tries to decide which AFTM-rated line he should buy. He may well remember that he should only aerialise 30 feet of line, but he still has the choice of either AFTM 7 or AFTM 8. He must also remember that a standard weight-forward line must only be aerialised as far as the end of the weight-forward section (30 feet).

As the line itself provides the weight which makes the rod work, it follows that more of a lighter line can be aerialised than a heavier line on a rod of a given rating. For example a DT5 line aerialised to say 40 feet might weigh about the same as a DT7 line aerialised to 30 feet. Therefore, if long casts are required with a DT line, our angler can buy a line of a lower AFTM rating, and aerialise more line in order to achieve his distance, provided of course that he has the distance *behind* him to permit long back casts.

A weight-forward line is not so flexible. Unless our angler buys a 'long-belly' line he is restricted to aerialising only 30 feet. Therefore, in order to get the best out of his fly line, he must select a line of a higher rating. In the case of an AFTM 7–8 rod he should select a WF8 line in order to obtain the rod compression that he requires to shoot the running line on the forward cast. A competent caster may even select a WF9 line.

Our angler must consider very carefully just what he wants his fly line to do. If he wants to fish close in to the margins he may well have a problem. He can stand further back from the bank and aerialise a reasonable amount of line if he has the room, or he can cast along the bank if no-one is near him. Either way he can aerialise enough line to make the rod work properly. If however, he is continually casting a short line, it will be necessary for him to invest in a heavier line which will compress the rod when less than 30 feet of it is aerialised.

If our angler casts long distances but requires good presentation, he may well have to use a DT line one or even two ratings lighter than his rod stipulates. Here though he must bear in mind just how much room he will have behind him to cast.

Remember that to cast effectively you must aerialise just enough line to make the rod work properly. Casting technique governs to a large extent which AFTM rating of line is most suitable, and this is why it is so important to test a complete outfit before buying it. Badly matched tackle is of no use to anyone, even though the rod and line might be the best that money can buy. We all accept that it is possible to get by, using tackle that may not be perfectly suited to the job in hand. However, it is for our own benefit to ensure that we get the best we can to cope with the general conditions that we are likely to encounter during our fishing.

There remains one more type of line which is becoming increasingly popular with stillwater trout anglers. The shooting head was devised a number of years ago in order to enable the angler to cast further. This is still the main purpose of the line, but it has now been developed for very deep lure fishing where presentation is just as important as distance.

The shooting head is really a development of the weight-forward line. As the name implies, the angler shoots the head and does not rely on aerialising the line to achieve distance. Initially shooting heads were 30 feet long, just the same as the weight-forward section of a fly line. The head is joined to a thin backing or shooting line; the angler aerialises the head and relies on the weight of the head to draw shooting line through the rod rings on the final forward cast. It is even more important with a shooting head to only aerialise the head, as it is impossible to control a shooting head if any amount of backing is aerialised as well. With a weight-forward line you can get away with aerialising *some* of the running line although it is not good policy to do so.

The rating of a shooting head is therefore of prime importance as the angler has no leeway at all to adjust the amount of line that he can aerialise. The best policy is to buy a shooting head equal to the higher rod rating. An AFTM 8 shooting head for an AFTM 7–8 rod. However, trial and error will tell you which rating is absolutely perfect. Without doubt, the best method of ensuring that you have a perfectly matched shooting head is to make it yourself.

Firstly, decide which kind of shooting head you require: floating, intermediate, slow sink, medium sink, or fast sink. Then purchase a double-taper line equal to the higher rating of your rod. Cut the line in half and sell the other half to a friend. You will now be left with a 15 yard shooting head. This needs to be cut back, but before you do this go out to an area of grass and aerialise the line. Start with 10 yards outside the tip ring and gradually extend or shorten the line outside the ring until you feel that the rod and line are working perfectly. Do not be in too much of a hurry to cut the line. Just make sure that the amount of line outside the tip ring is working the rod properly, and that you feel absolutely comfortable when handling it. You will probably find that you have between 11 and 12 yards of line outside the tip ring when you have finished. When you are completely satisfied mark the line 3 or 4 inches inside the tip ring and cut it at that point. You will now have a shooting head matched perfectly to your rod.

The next step is to select and join the shooting line to the shooting head. There are basically four types of backing:

1. Ordinary nylon monofilament 20–25 lb breaking strain. A fluorescent line such as Stren is very popular.
2. Flat nylon monofilament 20–25 lb breaking strain. Preferred

by many anglers as it does not tangle so easily nor bed in on the spool. Cortland Cobra (a red colour) is favourite.

3. Braided Dacron 15–30 lb breaking strain, preferred because of its suppleness and resistance to kinking. Cortland Micron Casting is well liked.

4. Braided monofilament 20–25 lb breaking strain is becoming very popular due to its low stretch factor and smooth finish which helps casting distance. The Gold Medallion line has an excellent reputation.

There are various methods of joining the shooting head to the running line, but whichever method you decide to use, please make sure that it is both secure and smooth enough to pass through the rod rings smoothly.

Both ordinary and flat nylon monofilament can be joined by the well tried and tested needle knot. (This is also the knot that can be used to attach leader butts to fly lines.) Firstly cut an end of the monofilament at an angle to leave a point. Now borrow a darning needle and push it half an inch up inside the fly line, ensuring that it goes up the centre of the braided core. Push the needle partway out through the plastic coating of the fly line and leave it there whilst you gently heat the pointed end with a match. The heat will melt the fly line coating sufficiently to leave a hole when the needle is removed. Now insert the pointed end of the nylon into the core of the fly line and out of the hole left by the needle. Pull about 4 or 5 inches of nylon through the hole. Make five turns of nylon around the fly line, returning the end of the nylon to where it comes out of the fly line thus forming a loop. Lay the end of the nylon along the fly line facing up the line towards the turns that you have just made. Now, using the loop in the opposite direction whip the nylon over both the fly line and the nylon tag. The nylon turns up the fly line will unwind as you make the turns over the tag. Make sure that all the turns of nylon fit snugly together, and that the joint is secure, than pull firmly on both the nylon and the shooting head to secure the knot properly. A small drop of Super Glue will secure the knot and a thin smear of Araldite over the whole joint will make it both smooth and waterproof.

The needle knot is probably the best method of attaching a monofilament butt to the end of the fly line. It produces a much slimmer joint than conventional knots, and permits the use of long leaders as it can be retrieved through the rod rings when netting a fish. Conventional joints do have a habit of stopping against rod rings which can cause a break when a fish makes a last dash for freedom.

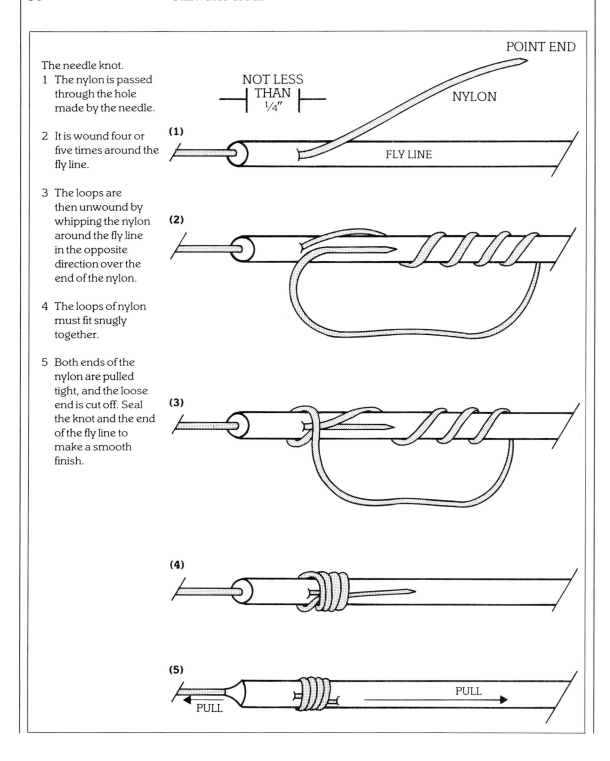

The needle knot.
1 The nylon is passed
   through the hole
   made by the needle.

2 It is wound four or
   five times around the
   fly line.

3 The loops are
   then unwound by
   whipping the nylon
   around the fly line
   in the opposite
   direction over the
   end of the nylon.

4 The loops of nylon
   must fit snugly
   together.

5 Both ends of the
   nylon are pulled
   tight, and the loose
   end is cut off. Seal
   the knot and the end
   of the fly line to
   make a smooth
   finish.

POINT END

NOT LESS
THAN
1/4"

NYLON

(1)

FLY LINE

(2)

(3)

(4)

(5)

PULL

PULL

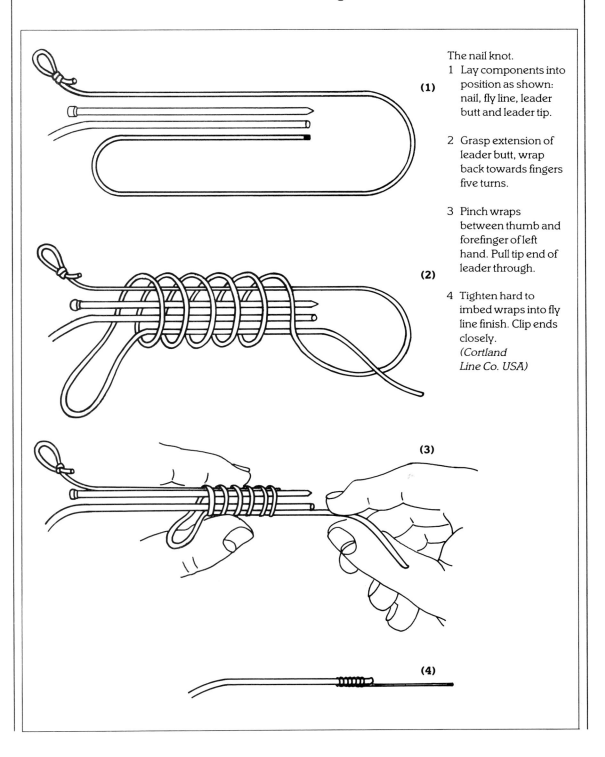

The nail knot.

(1)
1 Lay components into position as shown: nail, fly line, leader butt and leader tip.

2 Grasp extension of leader butt, wrap back towards fingers five turns.

(2)
3 Pinch wraps between thumb and forefinger of left hand. Pull tip end of leader through.

4 Tighten hard to imbed wraps into fly line finish. Clip ends closely.
(Cortland Line Co. USA)

(3)

(4)

Braided nylon and Dacron shooting lines can be attached to the shooting head by means of a splice. Dip the butt end of the shooting head into a bottle of cellulose thinners to a depth of about 1½ inches for a short time to soften the vinyl coating, then remove the coating with your fingernail. This will leave the core of the fly line exposed. A fine needle is inserted into the core of the braided shooting line for about one inch, and is then pushed through the side of the braid. The core of the fly line is threaded through the eye of the needle, and is then pulled through the braided shooting line by the needle until at least half an inch is outside the wall of the braid. Super Glue or quick-setting epoxy is used to secure the splice, and the ends are neatly trimmed. I then like to whip fly-tying silk along the whole of the splice and to give it one or two coats of varnish to make it waterproof.

There is a lot to consider when purchasing a fly line, but it must be remembered that with careful use a good fly line can last for years. It will last longer if it is used on a suitable rod. The selection of the correct density, profile and weight will certainly make your fishing both more enjoyable and successful.

Chapter 6

Your choice of reel

All fly reels are basically the same shape, and do the same job. They are all centrepin reels, which means that the spool revolves around a spindle, are usually made of metal but recently of either carbon or plastic. During the last few years reels have improved dramatically with tremendous reductions in weight, and improvements in drag systems.

Many stillwater anglers regard the reel as something to carry the line. This is almost true where anglers fight their fish by hand, but the quality and design of the reel play a large part when the fish is fought on the reel.

There are various points to look for when buying a reel. Firstly one must consider the size. Ideally a reel will hold the fly line plus at least 50 yards of backing. The backing fulfils two functions. It effectively lengthens the fly line should a fish take the fly immediately after the cast, and it allows the angler to let the fish run the fly line off the reel if necessary. The backing also builds up the spool, increases the rate of retrieve, and reduces the number of coils of fly line on the reel. Fly lines have a good memory, and lines put on a spool without backing will not shoot as well as a line with larger, looser coils.

The vast majority of manufacturers state the capacity of their reels together with an approximate guide to the amount of backing required. If, like me, you require the spool of your reels almost full, there is a very easy way of ensuring that you put enough backing on the spool. It is however easier if you buy two spools which would probably be the case with a new reel anyway.

Firstly wind the fly line evenly on to the spool, then attach the backing to the fly line. Now wind the backing on to the spool until it is full. Fit your second spool to your fly reel, attach the backing to the spool, and wind the backing and the fly line on to the second spool. Under normal circumstances 50 yards of backing is enough, but if the reel is for some reason very large, more backing can be used to build up the spool.

The size of the reel also affects the weight, and it is good policy to use the lightest reel that you can. There is however one very important factor to be borne in mind regarding weight. It is no good purchasing an ultra-light reel where the manufacturer has not only reduced the weight, but has reduced the strength as well. Plastic, in various forms, and carbon are now widely used in reel production, but the change from metals to plastic is not just a simple matter of change in material. Carbon and many plastics are brittle and very susceptible to damage if they come into contact with anything hard such as a rock or a size ten boot. Both materials can be susceptible to wear, and are not so easy to lubricate as metals. It is therefore necessary to ensure that the reel is not only light but strong, and it is worth sacrificing a little weight in order to ensure that your reel will last a reasonable time.

Having dealt with size and weight, we must now consider the design of the reel itself.

The spool

This must be removable in a simple operation in order that a replacement spool carrying an alternative line can be fitted easily and quickly should it be necessary. It must be polished both on the inner surface and the rim to ensure that there are no sharp edges to damage either the fly line or your fingers. Spare spools must be easily available as an accessory so that spares can be purchased to accommodate different lines. It is better that the outer rim is exposed in order that the angler can use finger pressure to control a

(Right) A reel with full rim control. *(Left)* A fully caged reel controlled only by the ratchet.

running fish. The spool should fit the spindle with very little free play, and only the smallest of gaps should appear between the spool and the cage. Should a large gap be present, it is more than likely that your line will jam in that gap at a crucial moment.

The case

This must be strong enough to stand up to knocks without cracking or distorting. The controls must be easy to operate in the coldest weather when your fingers are virtually numb. The case should be fitted with some form of line guide to direct the line on to the spool. Most importantly, the reel feet must be of a size to fit snugly into the reel fitting on the rod in order to avoid the reel working loose or twisting round whilst you are fishing.

The ratchet

This must be easily adjustable to suit the breaking strain of the leader in use. It must also be easily changed from left- to right-hand wind or vice versa. The ratchet must run smoothly to avoid jerking (which could break a light leader) and must be resistant to wear, this component being more susceptible to wear than any other part of the reel.

Drag system

This must increase pressure with each click of the mechanism; however it must leave the reel almost free-running when turned to the minimum setting. It must apply pressure evenly, and not pay out line in fits and starts. Most importantly, the drag system must

(Left) A fully caged reel fitted with a ratchet. (Right) A rim control reel fitted with a brake pad clutch system.

not be subject to high inertia. This is a common fault. Many reels have drag systems that work perfectly well once they are moving, but the pressure required to move the spool in the first place can be up to three times as much as the pressure required to turn the spool after it has begun to move. This high inertia can cause a break in the leader even though the drag is set correctly.

When purchasing a reel make sure that it will:

(a) hold the line plus at least 50 yards of backing.
(b) balance the rod.
(c) last a reasonable length of time.
(d) be possible to buy spare spools.
(e) be possible to purchase replacement parts if required.
(f) suit your style of fishing.

There are many fly reels available today; indeed, the angler is spoilt for choice when you consider how limited fly-reel design is. It is well to remember that fly reels were initially designed in Britain, and there are still very good reels made in the UK at reasonable cost. Hardy, Youngs, and British Fly Reels all make excellent ranges of reels at varying prices.

The one aspect of fly fishing where standard reels may not be of much assistance is when using shooting heads. The standard fly reel has a very small diameter arbour which makes line retrieval slow, and also puts very tight coils into backing. The tight coils in the backing cause loss of casting distance and tangles, both of which lead to less effective fishing.

Many anglers who specialise in shooting-head fishing have reverted to the old coarse-fishing centre-pin-type reel which has a much larger inside diameter to the spool. This means that less backing is required which reduces weight, the coils are larger and not so tight, and retrieval is much faster.

Bob Church has taken the matter a stage further by developing his Line Shooter reel specially for shooting-head work. Other anglers use reels such as the Match Aerial. Here again, make sure that the ratchet or drag is efficient, and if you are buying a second-hand reel, make sure that it is in good working order.

Chapter 7   **Accessories**

Having dealt with rods, reels and lines, it is necessary to deal with other items that the angler will require before he or she goes fishing.

Comfort is of paramount importance when fishing. If you are too hot or too cold you will not fish well. If your clothes are too tight they will restrict your casting. Let us start at the top. A hat is a vital necessity. Up to 60 per cent of body heat can be lost through the head, so a good hat will prevent such a loss and thus help to keep you warm. Conversely, a hat will protect your head from the sun. A peak at the front will both shade and protect the eyes, and a peak at the back will protect the neck against sun, rain, and low-flying insects. I prefer a tweed 'fore-and-aft' style of hat which, whilst not fully waterproof, has sufficient insulation to combat both high and low temperatures.

Polaroid glasses are a must. They reduce glare, permit you to see into the water to spot fish, and protect the eyes when casting. The alternative to Polaroids are the new Reactolite glasses which darken as light intensity increases. They do not however reduce glare as well as Polaroids.

Next we come to the upper body. A good heavy cotton shirt, a woollen crewneck jumper and a towelling cravat are my mainstays, all in either green or brown. I also wear a fishing waistcoat of green gaberdine. A good waistcoat with plenty of pockets is worth its weight in gold. When travelling light, all the accessories can be put in the pockets. Make sure that your waistcoat has rod loops so that you can change flies or make adjustments without having to put the rod down. It should also have a ring for the landing net hook, a patch of sheepskin or its synthetic equivalent for storing wet flies, and a smaller ring to which you can attach a lanyard to carry a pair of small scissors. The garment should be lightweight, and a loose but comfortable fit. Colour is not important as long as the angler can blend into the background. Avoid light colours such as white, yellow, orange, and blue.

A good warm waterproof coat is a necessity. I prefer a Barbour Solway Zipper, and wear a fleecy lining under it in cold weather.

Avoid nylons and plastics; these do not appear to have adequate ventilation. They can make you perspire both in summer and winter, and condensation forms inside the garment. One tip, should you purchase a jacket with a hood which is fixed by popper studs. To avoid the risk of loss, a few blobs of Super Glue will keep the hood in place.

The lower body tends to feel the cold more, and is not quite so easy to protect. Avoid denim and cotton trousers in cold, wet weather; they do not retain enough heat. Worsted or corduroy trousers are best as they will retain heat even when wet. In severely cold weather thermal underwear can work wonders but if you cannot justify this expense, a pair of lady's tights do a magnificent job. Make sure that the lady is out of them first, and remember to visit the smallest room before you leave home. I carry a pair of

(Left) Cold weather clothing for the angler. Note the hat, sunglasses, towelling cravat and mittens. *(Right)* Warm weather gear for the angler. Good socks soak up perspiration inside wellingtons. Note the use of the rod loops fitted to the waistcoat and the scissors attached to a lanyard. *(Photo: Andrew Gooding)*

Dunloproof over-trousers in a jacket pocket in case of rain.

Wellingtons are the normal footwear of all anglers. Make sure that they are plenty big enough, taking into account that one thin pair of socks and one good long woollen pair will be worn. Never wear Wellingtons without a good pair of woollen socks; these absorb the moisture which collects inside the boots. Also make sure that they have a good tread on them. I rely on rubber soles, and have not found a need for studded boots. Whatever you do, never wear waders when in a boat. If for some reason you end up in the water, the waders can trap air and you will end up floating upside down.

I find it almost impossible to fish in gloves. However, I do use mittens which have string palms and woollen backs. I find no difficulty in wearing a mitten on my casting hand, but do not like to wear one on my retrieving hand. I have yet to try a pair of palmless mittens, which at least protect the back of the hand and the fingers against the wind and rain. They would certainly appear to be a good investment.

The only other material item I take fishing with me is a towel. This is a towelling bar cloth kindly donated by my local landlord, and is a most useful item. It helps me to avoid spreading fish slime over my tackle. Also, in cold weather, it is most important to keep one's hands as dry as possible.

Now, having dressed for the part, and at least looking like anglers, we must consider the rest of the equipment that we require. Before we buy anything else, we must have something to put it all in. We therefore require a trout bag. There are many designs to choose from, but bear in mind that the bag must be large enough to carry all your accessories *and* your lunch. It does not, however, have to be large enough to carry your fish. The requirements are:

(a) It must be waterproof.
(b) Have an adjustable shoulder strap at least one inch wide.
(c) Be fitted with a ring for the landing-net hook.
(d) Have large divisions to contain reels, fly boxes, etc.
(e) Have two smaller divisions for nylon and for smaller accessories.

Make sure that the flaps adequately cover all the pockets to prevent the rain getting in, and ensure that the bag is made of a material which is hard wearing. A good average size is 17 inches long by 13 inches deep. The width is usually 4 or 5 inches.

The other accessories that you will require are:

Scissors – small, sharp, pointed ends, stainless steel.

Priest – to administer the *coup de grâce*.

Marrow spoon – to examine stomach contents of caught trout.

Forceps – to remove flies from deeply hooked fish.

Mucilin – to grease leader for dry fly or sub-surface nymphs. Do not use mucilin to grease fly lines as it can damage the plastic coating of the line.

Fly line cleaner – to remove dirt from line and maintain its floating qualities.

Sinking compound – usually a paste made up of washing-up liquid and Fuller's Earth to ensure that the leader sinks.

Dry fly dressing – to waterproof dry flies and ensure that they float.

Nylon spools – to make up leaders 4 lb, 5 lb, 6 lb, 8 lb, 9 lb breaking strain.

Supply of **ready-made leaders** such as the Normark Adapta Leader.

I purchase new nylon every season. Depending upon the amount that I am likely to use, I purchase it in either 25- or 50-yard spools. The 25-yard thumb spools are ideal as they can be fitted into a dispenser which keeps them neat and tidy.

Due to the fact that stillwater anglers tend to use long leaders, the standard tapered leaders, with or without droppers, are not really suitable. The only tapered leader suitable is the Normark Adapta. This 5-metre leader of tapered monofilament is available in three breaking strains of 3 lb, 5 lb, and 7 lb, and can be cut at either end to produce the exact leader that is required. A chart enclosed with

Contents of the author's tackle bag. Leaders, leader material, floatant, sinking compound, marrow spoon, priest, hook sharpener, leader straightener, and three fly boxes, plus a bar towel from 'you know who'.

each leader indicates the breaking strain at various points along the leader. We will deal more thoroughly with leaders later.

Another item of equipment that you will require is a landing net. Here again, many shapes and sizes are available. Do not buy a small net. Although it may be easy to carry, you will have problems getting a fish into it. Triangular nets are the most popular, and are certainly the easiest to use. The head should measure not less than 18 inches along the straight edge and preferably be 22 inches. The net itself should be reasonably deep, and do try to find a mesh that is of reasonable size. Hooks tend to get caught up in a fine mesh, hence the saying, 'What a mesh to get in'. The head of the net should fold down towards the handle which should be telescopic. Ideally the handle should extend to at least 30 inches, but if you plan a lot of boat fishing then a net with a 5-foot handle might well be necessary. Make sure that your net is fitted with a clip in order that it can be fixed to your belt, or to the loop on your trout bag, and then be easily released. There is nothing worse than trying to disengage a net from your person whilst fighting a trout. Mind you, it proves excellent entertainment for spectators.

I carry three fly boxes. The largest contains lures. It is made of wood, lined with ethafoam, and has proved to be totally satisfactory. The lures are easy to get at and the ethafoam repels water and inhibits rust forming on the hooks. The second box contains wet flies. It is double-sided and lined with foam which has parallel slots running along it. The hooks are pushed into the slots, and are held tight without the hackles being either crushed or bent. My third box contains nymphs, and is made by Efgeeco. It is a small double-sided box with strips of foam laid in it. The hooks are pushed into the foam strips and are held secure. The main benefit of this type of box is that air can circulate around the nymphs to dry them off.

Avoid fly boxes that attract or hold moisture as they will shorten the life of your flies. Also avoid boxes that are liable to distort either hackles or tails, or those boxes that are liable to break if they are dropped.

It can be argued that one large box would be better, but I find it easier to keep small boxes tidy; indeed, two of my boxes are pocket size. A large box means that you will *always* have to carry your trout bag, and there are times when this is downright inconvenient. Make sure that your boxes are fitted with reliable hinges and latches, and bear in mind that it may well be of benefit if they float.

One of the most important items of your equipment is the bag that you will keep your fish in. If you are going to the trouble and expense of catching your own fish, you owe it to yourself to get them home in the best condition possible. You therefore need a bag that can be left in the water; one which will allow the water to circulate around the fish. The old trout bass is still available and very popular, but today very good bags are made of synthetic materials. Make sure that the bass you buy is deep enough to contain a decent bag of fish, has strong handles, and will not suffer from prolonged immersion in water.

Whatever you do, do not keep fish in polythene bags. I was once fishing at Queen Mother Reservoir on a warm, sunny day. At the end of the day I weighed in four or five decent fish in prime condition. The angler after me weighed in the remains of one fish that he had kept in a polythene bag on the seat of his boat. It was beautifully cooked, but smelt rather funny. You have been warned.

A word on safety. Each year we hear of anglers being drowned, usually at sea. Accidents do happen, and if you are a regular boat angler I do suggest that you purchase a flotation jacket. The Heron and Quadrant jackets are both slim and comfortable; neither are expensive, but could save your life.

That then is a list of accessories that you will require in order to enjoy your trout fishing. You might like to add one or two other items such as a few plasters in case of minor mishaps, a can of insect repellant to keep away those midges, a temporary repair kit for boots and waders, and a handy, easy-to-use camera to record your successes.

Chapter 8

Basic casting technique

The one thing that commonly lets fishermen down, or deters people from taking up fly fishing, is casting. For some reason over recent years we appear to have got involved in a great deal of scientific nonsense about casting which has evolved into a mystery almost equal to that surrounding dry fly fishing on chalk streams.

Casting is basically the correct application of power to make the rod shoot line forward. Notice that I say, 'make the rod'. It is the rod that does the work for you, provided of course that your tackle is well balanced and suitable for the purpose to which it is being applied.

To my knowledge, two books have been written on the subject of casting, therefore to work within the limitations of this book I do not propose to dwell on the intricacies of technical know-how. Better to lay down the basic rules, and offer a valid explanation of why these rules exist.

The grip

Previously I have described the rod as a spring which propels the line back and forth. A spring requires a firm base which will hold it in place in order that it can build up power along its length. The grip must therefore be very firm, and resist flexing. There are two grips which I use: one for distance casting and one for shorter, accurate casts.

Should you visit a casting school, it is highly likely that you will be told that the casting action is very much like hammering a nail into a wall. The hammer grip is the universal grip for all types of casting. It is very firm, but permits controlled movement of the wrist which has to be applied at the end of both the forward and the backward cast.

The thumb grip is basically the same as the hammer grip, but the ball of the thumb is placed up the handle to give added support. This grip lessens the wrist movement, and aids casting accuracy, but reduces casting distance. I find it extremely useful when casting upwind of a rising fish as I can feel the rod bending under strain, and am therefore able to time my cast better in order to obtain improved presentation.

On no account should the index finger be extended up the handle. It restricts casting action, and can become very sore. There are no benefits to be gained by using this grip.

Casting aids

The vast majority of novices tend to flex the wrist too much during casting which reduces the power imparted to the line by the rod. It is

The hammer grip.

The thumb grip.

very common for anglers who have this problem to be advised to stick the butt of the rod under their coat cuff in order to keep it close to the wrist, thus reducing wrist movement. A Velcro wrist strap can help solve the problem of wrist movement – very simple to make and comfortable to wear. As well as helping beginners, it can be of permanent assistance to anglers whose wrists are not perhaps as strong as necessary, especially ladies and younger people.

A wrist strap is used to help support the wrist.

The wrist is locked at the commencement of the cast so that the arm can exert the power.

The basic principles

The whole idea of casting is to propel your fly forward as far as is necessary to catch fish. This might be 10 feet or 100 feet, perhaps even further, but the basic principles are the same. The rod must be used as a spring to propel the line forward at such a speed that the line's own momentum will pull more line out behind it, and thereby obtain the necessary distance. There are no weights to increase the momentum, only the weight of the line itself, and this must be used to the full.

The stance

In order to cast properly you must have an easy, comfortable stance which permits unrestricted movement of the body. Therefore it is not advisable to stand square on to the direction in which you

(Left) The basic cast. The angler is well balanced. The left hand keeps tension on the line. The rod is almost vertical, and the elbow is close to the body. The wrist has allowed the rod to drift back slightly with the line. *(Right)* The standard cast as seen from the rear.

intend to cast. It is better to stand at an angle of between 30 and 50 degrees to the casting direction so that you are in fact casting across your body to a certain extent. This permits the transfer of weight from the front foot to the back one. Obviously your stance will depend on the condition of the bank on which you are standing, but it is important to be as comfortable as possible.

The back cast

In order to attain sufficient line speed, and to ensure a good loop, the back cast is of ultimate importance. To start the back cast, the forearm should be parallel to the ground, or at a nine o'clock position. The upper arm should be close to your side. The rod itself must be a direct continuation of the arm. Keeping the wrist straight will ensure that the handle of the rod is touching the underside of the wrist.

The initial movement is a firm upward one of the lower arm to

At the top of the cast. The rod has been allowed to cock the wrist slightly which will help to start the forward cast.

1   The initiation of the back cast. The rod is under compression lifting the line from the water. The angler's forearm is already in the vertical position.

2   The initiation of the forward cast. The rod is under compression, and the angler's arm is moving downwards. Note the straight line from the rod tip.

3   The forward cast. The angler has stopped the rod at 10 o'clock and the line is unfolding well above the water so that it will land delicately, and in a straight line.

the twelve o'clock position followed by a very small movement of the wrist to accommodate the momentum of the rod which will carry through to the one o'clock position.

At this stage it is important to stop any further backward movement which would result in the line losing speed, forming a wide loop, and dropping behind you.

The stop

As I have already mentioned, the rod acts as a spring. On the back cast you will see the rod bend downwards under tension. As the line flies out behind you, this tension will reduce and the rod will straighten. As the line straightens behind you, the tension will be increased in the opposite direction, and the rod will begin to bend backwards. In order to achieve a good cast the 'stop' is most important, as you must give the line time to put the rod under tension in order to put the spring into effect on the forward cast.

Novice casters tend to worry as they extend more line, that it will drop behind them; consequently their casting action gets faster and faster. Eventually the line will be going in the opposite direction to the rod, and all the power will be lost. In truth, the action of the rod may well increase in speed as more power is applied; however, the length of the 'stop' will increase in a direct ratio to the length of the line which is being aerialised. The timing of the 'stop' is the most important part of the cast, and this alone will dictate the length of your cast.

The forward cast

The forward cast is not, as some people think, the direct opposite of the back cast. The initial movement is certainly similar in that the forearm moves downwards from the one o'clock position, but in order to apply power for the distance cast, the upper arm moves forward. The lower arm will stop at ten o'clock. If the downward movement is continued past this point, the line will not be able to complete the forward loop before it hits the water. The wrist, which you remember was slightly cocked at the end of the back cast, is finally uncocked to add a final flick of power to the forward cast to help extend line.

Extending line

Earlier I mentioned that rods were designed to work best with 30 feet of similarly rated line extended. This is all well and good, but there is no doubt that you will want to cast further than 30 feet; and you will also retrieve line so that there is less than 30 feet extended past the rod tip. In both cases it will be necessary to either extend line by false casting or to shoot line.

False casting is the term used by anglers when they are going through the complete casting motion without permitting the line to settle on the water. There are two reasons for false casting. One is to dry a dry fly, the other is to extend line. After retrieving a cast it is necessary to extend the line again before casting a second time. The false cast is the only answer, and this is where many people get the idea that fly fishing is a matter of swishing a rod about a lot. The false cast is identical to the full cast except that the line is allowed to shoot through the rod guides on the forward cast, then gripped again before it touches the water when the rod is taken again into the back cast. Remember that the line is always extended only on the forward cast. To extend line on the back cast means a loss of power, and a search amongst the bushes and grass behind you for lost flies. To my mind it is bad manners and bad technique to strip line directly from the reel when false casting to extend line. It is a much better idea to strip the necessary length of line from the reel before commencing to cast. The repetitious screech of a reel giving line when false casting certainly gets on my nerves, and I doubt if I am alone in my reactions.

Shooting line

The final act of the cast is to shoot line to achieve the distance required. The quality of the casting action and the balance of the tackle will dictate the amount of line which will shoot through the guides. The shoot is almost the same as the motion of extending line on the false cast – the line is permitted to slide through the fingers on the forward cast. Timing of the release is of utmost importance. It is necessary to release the line when the aerialised line is moving forward and has sufficient momentum to pull the line through the rod guides. Therefore the release will occur when the rod is in front of the angler. When casting to a specific fish it is best to aim about a yard above the point where you want the fly to land. To aim at a point on the water will mean a late release, and consequently a heavy landing which may well put the fish down.

Casting variations

In circumstances dictated by local geography, or more likely by the weather, it will be necessary to change the casting action. In a head wind, for example, it is necessary to cast low and under the wind. This may sound ridiculous, but it is a fact that there is less wind near the water surface. A low cast will therefore achieve greater distance. The casting movement is adapted to start lower and to finish lower.

In a back wind it is necessary to start the back cast higher, and to let the rod drift slightly further back than normal which will throw the line behind lower, getting under the wind. The forward cast is stopped higher, and the line is released earlier so that the wind can help achieve distance.

If you are fishing with a steep bank behind you, it will be necessary to throw the back cast higher. Therefore, the rod will start at a lower position, and finish at a position between eleven and twelve o'clock. The line will be thrown upwards and away from any obstructions.

There are other variations which you will gradually pick up as you go along, but remember that the basic cast is the basis of all good casting, and variations are only variations on the same theme.

A high back cast. The right arm is extended vertically, but the rod has not been allowed to go too far back. The left hand is by the angler's side, keeping the line under tension.

(1)   (2)   (3)

The double haul.

1 The angler starts the back cast.

2 As the back cast continues the angler pulls the line down with the left hand.

3 With his body turned side-on the angler can let the rod drift further back. The left hand is moving towards the rod.

4 The back cast is complete. The angler's left hand is level with the rod butt.

5 The forward cast. The angler's left hand has pulled the line down to increase line speed.

(4)   (5)

Some anglers and many tournament casters can reach distances in excess of 60 metres using shooting heads. This is not possible with full lines of course, where to put out a complete 30- or 35-yard line is a feat in itself.

Advanced casting

The tournament caster uses a cast which includes one or two additional movements to the basic cast. These additional movements are called hauls. The idea is to increase the tension the rod is under to make it bend further and thereby to increase line speed and casting distance.

This can become an involuntary movement of the free arm which develops naturally as the casting action improves. Basically it is a sharp pull on the line with the left hand as the rod begins the back cast. This pull releases the line from the water tension, and sets an early curve in the rod which results in the line being thrown faster to the rear. The faster line speed on the back cast sets a greater curve in the rod which will result in faster line speed forward, and greater distance. If you want to increase your casting distance, try this before going on to the double haul.

The single haul

As the name suggests, a second haul is used, this time as the rod starts the forward cast. It probably sounds peculiar that you are pulling line in with the left hand when in fact your sole aim is to achieve the greatest distance possible. However, what you are in fact doing is putting a greater curve into the rod in order that the spring effect will be greater and shoot your line further. This technique takes some mastering and practice is necessary, preferably away from the water so that you do not annoy other anglers.

The double haul

1. Learn to cast on grass.

A few tips

2. If you are right handed try to fish with the wind coming over your left shoulder. It keeps the line away from your face. Left handers vice versa.
3. If you feel a cast going wrong, STOP. You cannot adjust sufficiently to recover it.
4. Find someone to teach you the good casting habits; it is all too easy to pick up the bad ones.
5. Don't be discouraged. Remember that most trout are caught within 15 yards of the bank.
6. Rest frequently. A novice expends a lot of energy. Your casting will not improve if you are tired.
7. Remember that fishing is a hobby, and that you should enjoy it. Relax and take things easily.

Chapter 9

Lure fishing

Those anglers who decry lure fishing as a chuck-and-chance method are the same ones who only catch fish occasionally when using lures. Whilst it is generally agreed that lure fishing might not have the finesse of nymph fishing, or loch-style methods, the anglers who use lures successfully are just as skilful as their nymphing and loch-style counterparts.

Successful lure fishing has developed rapidly during the last few years. No longer can the chuck-and-chance label be tied to a method that now offers many variations in style, giving an almost endless permutation of presentations which would not have been thought of a few years ago. The Northampton anglers who fish Rutland and Grafham are to be thanked for their pioneering, methodical approach to new fishing methods, especially Bob Church and Steve Parton who have both written excellent books which are well worth reading.

As there are a number of books available for those anglers who wish to develop their lure-fishing skills, I will deal with basic lure fishing, and explain what I believe to be a successful, methodical approach. Method is of utmost importance when lure fishing, more so than when fishing any other method, because unless you fish methodically you will not be successful. Also if you *do* catch a fish, you will not be in a position to repeat the method accurately enough to catch another. Poor anglers can make lure fishing into a chuck-and-chance method. Good anglers can make you believe that anyone can do it, then prove differently.

Selection of lures

It is generally agreed that the most productive lures are either Black, White or Orange. By this I mean that the *predominant* colours are black, white or orange. Other colours may well be present as follows:

PREDOMINANTLY WHITE

Baby Doll	White
Appetiser	White, grey, red, green
Jack Frost	White, red

PREDOMINANTLY BLACK

Black Chenille	Black
Viva	Black, green, silver
Sweeney Todd	Black, red

PREDOMINANTLY ORANGE

Orange Leadhead	Orange
Whiskey Fly	Orange, gold
Church Fry	Orange, grey, gold

It is therefore necessary to carry a selection of lures in the three predominant colours.

The profile of the lure must also be taken into account as there are times when the fish require a secondary stimulation, for example:

WINGED LURES	HACKLED LURES	BODY & TAIL LURES
Appetiser	Jack Frost	Leadheads
Viva	Fuzzy Wuzzy	Baby Doll
Church Fry	Worm Fly	

The profile is often important when fish are feeding on fry. When a trout sees a lure above it, the profile is possibly the only stimulation, as the lure will appear a virtual silhouette.

The action of the fly will provide another stimulant. This, of course, can be varied by changes in the style of the retrieve. However, the positions of the hackles, the type of wing, and the size of the tail can be of importance.

SLIM WING	PULSATING WING
Matuka	Appetiser (Marabou wing)
Streamer	Christmas Tree (Marabou wing)

PULSATING HACKLE	PULSATING TAIL
Jack Frost	Leadheads
Worm Fly	

The remaining stimulant to be considered is the swimming characteristic of the lure. At times when the trout are surrounded by an abundance of food they become lazy, and need to be tempted even more to take a lure:

SINK & DRAW	FLOAT & DIVE
Leadheads	Dalberg Diver

Not so much a stimulant, but nevertheless a very important factor is the size of the lure. All too often one angler catches fish while his close neighbour on the bank does not. We have all experienced those days when fish pluck at the lure, but very few of them get hooked. A change of size rather than of pattern may well be the answer.

It follows therefore that an angler requires a good selection of lures in order to be able to ring the changes frequently should it be necessary.

There are two other factors which the angler must bear in mind.

The result of counting to control your depth. These two big fish of 5 lb 11 oz and 6 lb ½ oz were taken on consecutive casts at Upper Tamar Lake on a Viva after a count of 25 on a medium sink line.

Fish will congregate at a depth which suits them, be it for comfort **Depth**
or for easy pickings of food. It is unlikely that a trout will bother to
chase a lure which is being retrieved a long way above or below it.
Trout will not expend more energy chasing food forms than they
can gain from eating them.

Sometimes it appears that the faster a lure is stripped, the more fish **Speed of retrieve**
are caught. This may be true early in the season when there is a
predominance of stock fish, but later in the year it is a different
story. Here again, during the summer months when there is plenty
of food a trout will not bother to chase a lure doing twenty miles an
hour. Why should it? There are plenty of alternatives which are
easier to catch, and probably tastier to eat. Rate of retrieve must
therefore be adjusted until a suitable speed is found to be successful.

Some lures are designed to suit a certain style of retrieve. The
lead-headed lures, also known as crappie jigs, sink nose first. A
retrieve with a good pause will therefore make the lure rise and fall.
The Muddler, if tied with a good deer-hair head, will rise nose first.
It is usually fished on a sinking line with a good pause between
pulls and will behave in the opposite way to the lead head. The
Dalberg Diver will float when static. The deer-hair head is cut to
form a sloping profile which will pull the lure down when retrieved.
This can be very effective when fished on a long leader in conjunction
with a floating line.

A number of lures have been designed to imitate small fish and
other aquatic life. The ethafoam floating-fry lures are usually fished
static. They imitate fry stunned or killed by trout attacking a shoal.
The Ombudsman, designed by Brian Clarke, is termed a lure
mainly due to the fact that it is tied on a long shank eight or ten
hook. It was however designed to imitate an Alder larva, and
various caddis which are found around the lake bed. If this lure is
fished properly, the retrieve will be a slow figure of eight.

Lures designed to imitate small fish should be retrieved in such a
way that they in fact do just that. No fish swims at a steady pace in
the same direction at a constant depth. Variation is the answer. A
short pause between pulls will give a jerky motion, a long pause
will give a fluttering effect. Constant changes of pace throughout the
retrieve may stimulate a fish to strike.

Anglers fishing at Farmoor, Oxford developed the technique of
fishing round a curve. The cast was made, then the angler walked a
few paces along the bank before starting the retrieve. This put a
curve in the line which stimulated the fish, and also helped the
angler to cover more water.

Boat fishing

To my mind this is the most enjoyable way of fishing a lure. The variations in style and technique are virtually unlimited.

Anchored

Anglers select an area of water to fish, and use a selection of lures at various depths with various speeds of retrieve. If they are not successful, they move on and try somewhere else.

Advantages: Casting is almost always downwind. Control of the lure is easy.

Disadvantages: Anglers are sometimes unwilling to move on, and will wait for fish to come to them.

Notes: The boat should be anchored nose downwind, one angler fishing downwind to the right, and the other downwind to the left. The angler in the front of the boat has priority when casting. For right-handed anglers, the front angler casts to the left, and the rear angler casts to the right. This keeps the lines away from each other, and ensures a good coverage of the water.

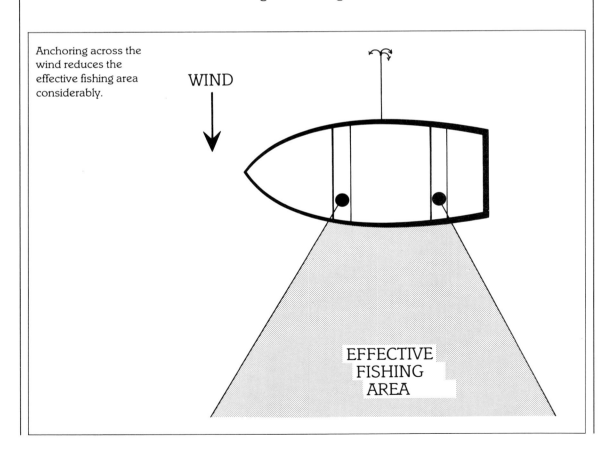

Anchoring across the wind reduces the effective fishing area considerably.

WIND

EFFECTIVE
FISHING
AREA

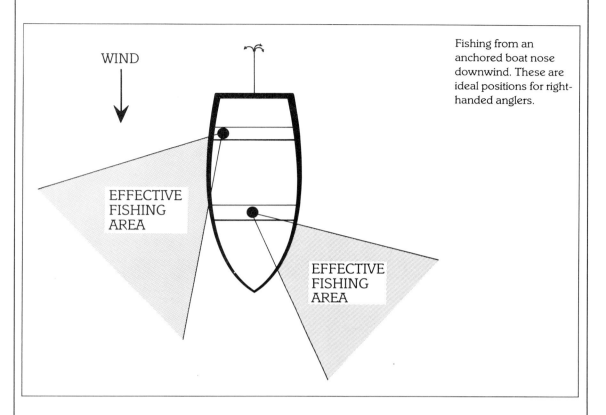

WIND

EFFECTIVE
FISHING
AREA

EFFECTIVE
FISHING
AREA

Fishing from an
anchored boat nose
downwind. These are
ideal positions for right-
handed anglers.

Side-swiping

The boat is drifted nose downwind either on the rudder to give directional control, or on a stern-mounted drogue.

Advantages: More water is covered on the drift. The lure is fished in a curve.

Disadvantages: This method limits the angler to fishing the upper layers of the water.

Notes: The anglers cast at an angle between 90 and 45 degrees to the rear of the boat, one on either side. Usually slow or medium sink lines are used. The lure is retrieved almost immediately, and fished around the curve created by the forward movement of the boat. Takes can come at any time, but are more likely when the lure increases speed around the final curve to come up in line behind the boat. The final movement of the lure is to go up through the water and around the curve, an action which trout find hard to resist. When using this method there is only a little time in which you can permit the lure to sink before starting the retrieve, otherwise the presentation is lost. Therefore the lure can only be fished in the top 2 or 3 feet of water.

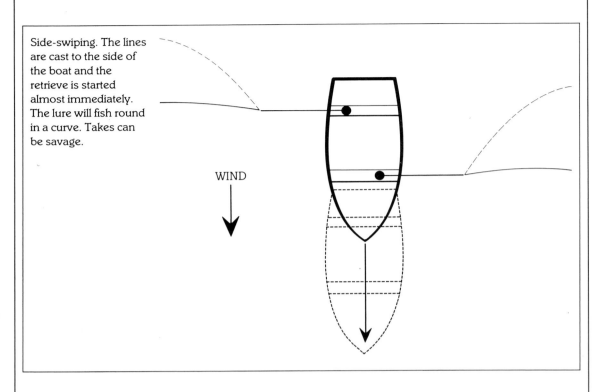

Side-swiping. The lines are cast to the side of the boat and the retrieve is started almost immediately. The lure will fish round in a curve. Takes can be savage.

WIND

Northampton style

So named because it is the style for which the Northampton anglers are best known. The boat is drifted nose downwind on the rudder. Anglers, using shooting heads, cast 90 degrees to the side of the boat, and pay out line as the boat drifts. The line sinks straight down until the angler stops paying out line, when it straightens out and tightens behind the boat. The retrieve is usually slow as the drift speed of the boat has to be taken into account.

Advantages: All depths can be fished effectively. Rudder control helps the anglers to follow the bank and fish a chosen contour.

Disadvantages: Whilst being very effective, this can also be a slow-action type of fishing.

Notes: This is a most effective method. However, it is necessary to ensure that the distance you cast and the amount of line you pay out are accurate. It is best that both anglers use identical tackle. Then when one of the anglers is successful he can tell his partner what method he has used. The depth that the lure is fished at is controlled by both the casting distance and the amount of line paid out. To fish deep, keep the cast short and pay out more. To fish shallow, cast further and pay out less. You must be able to give your partner accurate details such as, 'Cast 15 yards, pay out 20'.

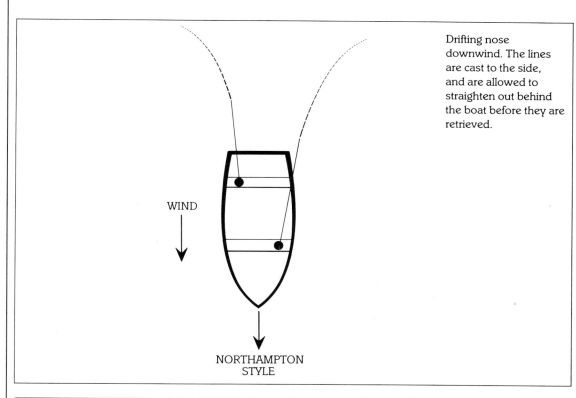

Drifting nose downwind. The lines are cast to the side, and are allowed to straighten out behind the boat before they are retrieved.

WIND

NORTHAMPTON
STYLE

The correct positions for right-handed anglers when drifting nose downwind.

With the variety of sinking-line densities now available it is possible to present a lure at virtually any depth you wish, and to search the water thoroughly.

You will realise that each of the foregoing methods ensures that anglers fish as much water as possible. In each case the anglers fish out of opposite sides of the boat, covering more water than is possible by either anchoring side-on to the wind, or by drifting side-on downwind. This is a deliberate policy as fish location is of utmost importance, especially when fishing unknown waters. Each method will prove best in certain situations. There will be times when the wind is too strong to drift; there will be other times when fish are moving upwind in the top layers; and there will also be times when fish are in isolated pockets of deep water. The angler must be able to read the water quickly and accurately in order to waste as little time as possible in locating the fish.

When the fish are found the angler must be in a position to cover them a second time. It is essential that he immediately mark his position from points on the bank. You can always make a guess, but if you are drifting a long way from the shore it is very easy to be 50 yards out in your calculation and miss the fish on the second drift. It is best to use the method tried and tested by sea anglers.

Take a mark on the bank that you are heading towards, e.g. a tree in line with a telegraph pole. Now take a mark on one of the banks to either side, e.g. a church tower in line with a hill top. When you have finished the successful drift, motor or row upwind being careful not to motor over your intended drift. Line up both your marks again, and you will fish the same drift.

Having ensured that you are fishing the same drift, you need to accurately repeat your fishing technique in order to stand more chance of catching the next fish. No doubt, having just caught a fish you will still have the same lure on your cast, and no doubt you will remember what speed of retrieve was successful. However, how will you determine the depth at which your lure took the fish? The answer is to count while your lure is sinking. Cast and count every time. This is the only way that you can search the water thoroughly.

I generally carry two densities of sinking lines: a Cortland No. 2 density, which I class as a medium-sink rate, and a Cortland No. 4 density, which is comparatively fast. Unless I know what my tactics will be on the day, I first use the No. 2 density line counting five on the first cast, and adding five per cast until I reach forty-five. If nothing has happened after trying the basic colour lures, I will switch to the No. 4 density line, counting fifteen on the first cast, increasing again by five per cast until I reach sixty, or the bottom.

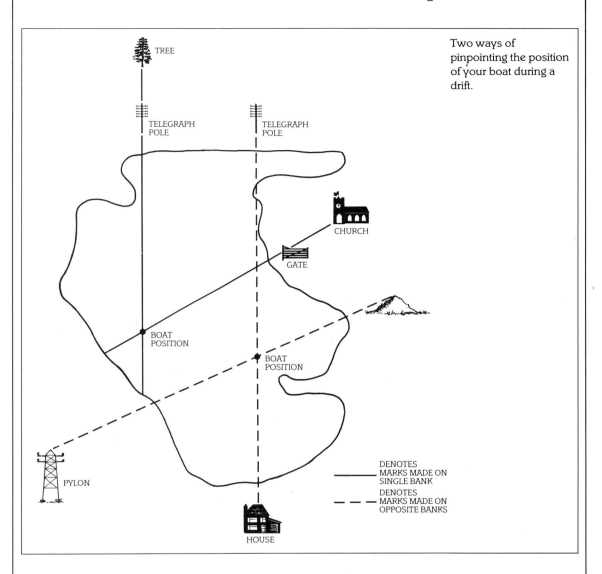

TREE

TELEGRAPH POLE

TELEGRAPH POLE

Two ways of pinpointing the position of your boat during a drift.

CHURCH

GATE

BOAT POSITION

BOAT POSITION

PYLON

DENOTES MARKS MADE ON SINGLE BANK

DENOTES MARKS MADE ON OPPOSITE BANKS

HOUSE

By using this method I can be sure that I have searched the water thoroughly.

I well remember a day at Upper Tamar Lake on the Devon–Cornwall border during May 1979. After a fruitless morning drifting around fishing nymphs, I anchored in deeper water about 70 yards from the dam. I was fishing a Viva on a Cortland No. 2 density line, and eventually took a stock fish after a count of twenty-five. I maintained the depth for two or three more casts, and latched into a big fish on the first pull of the retrieve. Ten minutes later I boated a rainbow of 5 lb 11 oz. I straightened the leader and cast again, counted to twenty-five, and hooked another fish on the first pull of the retrieve. Fifteen minutes later I boated my biggest trout ever – 6 lb ½ oz. If I had not bothered to count, my chances of boating such a tremendous double would have been very remote, but I knew my depth, and repeated the successful formula to lure another large trout.

Bank fishing

No doubt, this is the way that many of us started. Unfortunately some of us do not seem to progress past this stage, which is a great pity. However, fishing lures from the bank is a very productive method of fishing, accounting for many thousands of fish each season.

The main problem, especially with anglers new to the sport, appears to be an apparent unwillingness to move. Why this is, I just do not know; but anglers fishing lures from the bank seem to be permanently fixed to one spot. I can quote one good example of this apparent inability to move which occurred at Kennick Reservoir during the 1985 season. I went to the reservoir after work, and bought an evening ticket. There was an angler fishing an orange lead head on a section of bank known to the locals as Duffers Point. It was late in the afternoon, so I walked on up the bank and fished for a couple of hours, then walked back. Our angler was still fishing away on Duffers Point, and had in fact taken two fish on his lure.

The next day I again fished Kennick, and saw the same angler on Duffers Point. I fished through the day until teatime, and took a five-fish limit. As I walked back to the car I passed our angler. 'No luck today,' he said. 'Can't understand it. Caught two here yesterday.' He had fished the same lure in the same place for about eight hours without so much as a sign of a fish. What a waste of time and money. If only he had walked two hundred yards up the bank he would have found fish gorging themselves on damsel-fly nymph. Then again, would he have recognised the signs and known what to do?

Perhaps the unwillingness to move is derived from the habits of many coarse anglers who are prepared, and often compelled, to fish one swim all day. I must admit that it felt strange to walk around the reservoir with such a small amount of tackle when I took up trout fishing, but I certainly treated this change as an advantage.

The first rule of bank fishing is therefore to move, and to search the water for fish. It is useless to wait for the fish to come to you.

When bank fishing I take three lines with me: Cortland No. 1, 2 and 3 density. The Cortland 444 No. 2 density is my standard line, but it is often necessary to change to a No. 1 density for slow retrieves near the surface, or to the No. 3 density to fish a lure across the bottom. If your fishery has a rocky or snaggy bottom, you will find that your line selection is critical. A line with a fast sink rate will not permit you to fish a lure slowly as it will get snagged up before your retrieve is finished. It is then better to go for a lighter-density line where you might have to wait longer for the line to sink to the right depth, but at least you will be able to fish the lure right to the bank at a sensible speed.

There is no need to revert to the chuck-and-chance method when bank fishing. It pays to search the water thoroughly, working down through the layers with a variety of lures. Fish close-in first, then fan your casts out and around the water in front of you. Ideally, select a section of bank where the wind is behind and over your left shoulder if you are right handed. This will help your casting distance, and keep the line away from your face. Try to fish on a promontory where fairly deep water is within casting range. If the weather is cold early in the season, few fish will be found in the shallow water. Late in the season take a position near the entrance to feeder streams as these will attract fish feeding on fry as well as those feeling the urge to spawn. However, avoid these areas early in the season as it is likely that they will be populated by black fish.

Above all, fish the water methodically, remembering to count after each cast to help depth control. Bear in mind that trout often swim in shoals when freshly stocked. If you get a fish, cast out again as quickly as you can; there may well be a few more trout eager to accept your lure. Do not stay in one spot. It may be the only area of the water that for some reason is unsuitable for the trout at that particular time, and they will avoid it. Fish all the likely places that you can, bearing in mind the prevailing wind direction, also the wind direction for the previous three or four days. Fish will move upwind near the surface. Try lures of all the basic colours. Although we tend to have our favourites, do not be led into thinking that one lure is better than all the others. They all work on their day.

When lure fishing from bank or boat you can experience some pretty savage takes due to the speed that you are moving the lure. I must admit that I do not like elastic line between fly line and leader. I agree that it will absorb the shock from smash takes, but I like to feel every movement of the fish, and this is deadened by using elastic line. I therefore use a leader tapering down to 5 or 6 lb breaking strain for all my lure fishing. I really do not see any point in fishing with a heavier leader as you totally outclass the fish, and get little sport from the fight. Nor do I fish lighter than 4 lb breaking strain as I have no wish to leave a hook in a fish, and get no satisfaction from boasting about it if it does occur.

Lure fishing is a very exciting way of catching trout, especially since new methods of presentation have been developed. It should not be frowned upon by so-called purists, but conversely it should not be treated as the one and only method of catching trout. The various methods of lure fishing, particularly from a boat, take a considerable time to master and require just as much skill as any other method in the stillwater-angling scene.

Chapter 10   **Nymph fishing with floating lines**

I make no secret of the fact that nymph fishing is my favourite form of trout fishing. I find it demanding, exasperating, tiring, and totally absorbing. I also feel a sense of achievement on those occasions when I manage to take a limit. I tend to gloat when I have more fish on the nymph than the angler next to me who is stripping a lure, and I find it easier to make plausible excuses when I do not catch anything.

First of all it is necessary to define a nymph. A nymph is any one of the aquatic larval forms which make up part of the life cycle of a fly. For example, two stages in the life cycle of a sedge can be termed nymphs. They are the larva (stick fly) and the pupa. Also two stages in the life cycle of a buzzer can be termed nymphs. They are the larva (blood worm) and the pupa (commonly, but wrongly, called the buzzer).

The damsel and dragon flies have only one aquatic stage in their life cycle which is the nymph. The adult fly hatches out in the air after the nymph has climbed up the bank or up a reed. Some wholly aquatic animals can be termed nymphs due to the way that the artificials are fished. The shrimp is a prime example; the corixa, though not wholly aquatic, is another example.

You will appreciate therefore that there are many small forms of aquatic life upon which trout can feed. Thankfully our still waters each hold a selection of these nymphs, and it is therefore possible to narrow down your choice to perhaps half a dozen nymphs tied in two or three different sizes and perhaps two or three different colours.

It is generally accepted that nymph fishing is carried out with a floating line, and therefore that fish are taken from the top few inches of the water. This is often true, but to think no further than this can lead to disappointment. All nymphs in their early stages of growth grovel around on the bottom, feeding on waste matter and decaying vegetation. It is here amongst the plant growth and last year's leaves that they find both food and shelter. They are cold blooded, hibernating during the winter in most cases and only coming to life when the water temperature rises. The only time that they will venture to the surface is when they are ready to hatch into an adult fly. The timing of the hatch depends on the maturity of the nymph, the temperature of the water, and to some extent the temperature of the air. One must also remember that it takes more than one hatching nymph to cause a rise. It takes hundreds if not thousands.

To be a successful nymph fisherman it is necessary to read the water before making up your mind which method to use. Are fish rising, can you see the classic head and tail rise which generally means that trout are taking nymphs just under the surface? Can you see small sipping rises caused by trout taking small nymphs? If the answer is 'yes', then you can certainly use the floating line and fish just under the surface, but just how you do it will decide whether you have an average or a brilliant day.

Firstly we will look at methods of fishing the sub-surface nymph. An angler may cast to a fish that he has seen, *knowing* it to be there and feeding. He may however 'fish the water', which means that he will cast, *hoping* that a fish will be there.

It always amazes me the way some anglers march down to the water and cast as far as they can then, if rules permit, wade to within an inch of the top of their waders in order to cast even further. On a number of occasions, notably at Wimbleball and Church Hill Farm, I have caught trout when my fly line has been lying on the ground, and I have been about 10 yards away from the

The author fishes a nymph near the causeway at Kennick Reservoir.

water's edge. I appreciate that a fish's field of view lessens the nearer the creature gets to the surface, but if I can fish without letting it know that I am there, I feel that I have a better chance of success. It is important to realise that trout can find more food in the margins than they can in deeper water, provided of course that the food forms and plant life have not been killed off by anglers continually wading. Therefore it is good policy to search the shallow water before casting further. A fly line landing on the water, no matter how delicately it is cast, will spook fish swimming below it.

My general approach is to keep away from the bank, and to gradually extend the length of my cast in order to search the water thoroughly. If I am casting to rising fish I always cast to the nearest fish if I have a choice.

Nymphing trout generally move upwind. They do this so that food forms drift down towards them, and they do not have to expend much energy chasing them. A cast to a nymphing fish should always be made with an allowance in the upwind direction for fish movement, taking into account the time it will take for the nymph to sink to the correct depth and gain a natural attitude. Usually 6 to 10 feet is sufficient, and trout will move 4 or 5 feet to intercept a nymph.

With the fish so close to the surface, it is very easy to disturb them with poor casting or heavy tackle. Over recent years anglers have found it beneficial to use long leaders in order to keep the fly

A typical hook hold. This buzzer-caught trout had little chance of escape.

line away from the fly, and to help ensure that the nymph lands delicately. Leaders of up to 30 feet have been used, but I usually manage quite well with a leader of between 12 and 18 feet. In windy weather I use a shorter leader in order to keep control, and have found that the fish are not so easily disturbed as there are waves on the water anyway. A tapered leader with a point of between 3 and 6 lb breaking strain is ideal. I regularly use the Normark Adapta Leader which is approximately 16 feet of tapered monofilament which can be cut at both butt and tip to make a leader of the length and breaking strain required. A double-taper fly line helps with the delicate presentation, and a rod with a middle-to-tip action gives me good casting distance, fast strike reaction, and good fish control.

Fish can be particularly fussy when they are taking sub-surface nymphs. They become used to finding their food at a specific depth, and it is thus of the utmost importance that the angler presents his nymph at the correct depth. In some cases we may be talking of a depth of less than one inch, and it is in circumstances such as this that correct presentation is essential. Normally leaders are left ungreased, but when a slow retrieve is used the nymph will sink below the fish and will not be seen. A fully greased leader riding high on the water surface is easily seen by trout, and may well put them off. The answer is to apply floatant to the leader at regular intervals along its length to hold it up, but allow sections to

An angler uses natural cover to avoid detection.

sink below the surface and remain undetected. Try to avoid greasing the leader within 3 inches of the fly.

Sub-surface presentation

There are four basic methods of presentation to trout feeding sub-surface.

Static fishing

Often used when fishing buzzers or snail imitations in calm weather in the surface film. This eliminates the risk of 'V' wakes forming behind the fly line, leader knots, or the fly. The nymph is simply cast out and left for a fish to find it. A very simple and successful method if there are plenty of fish about.

Drift fishing

Virtually the same as static fishing, but used when there is a breeze strong enough to move the water surface. The nymph is cast slightly upwind, and allowed to drift downwind. This method gives excellent presentation, especially when the angler is fishing a wind lane running parallel to the bank. This method can also be used in strong winds, but the cast is made directly across the wind, and the nymph is permitted to fish down and around into the bank.

Figure of eight

The standard retrieve of nymph fishermen. The figure of eight is a constant, slow retrieve, the speed of which can be varied to suit prevailing conditions. The main advantage of this method is that the angler is always in close contact with the nymph, and can strike more quickly.

Stripping retrieve

This is a slower version of the lure retrieve, and is very useful as it moves the nymph spasmodically. The very nature of the retrieve makes the nymph alternate between fast and slow movements which will also slightly change the depth at which the nymph is being fished. Many takes will occur when the line is slack and the nymph is falling in the water.

   The speed and method of retrieve are very important. Remember that we are usually fishing specific imitations, and we must try to emulate the movement of the natural nymph. Trial and error eventually ascertain the best retrieve on the day.

The deep nymph

Fished effectively, the deep nymph can, over a period of a season, outfish the sub-surface nymph by quite a margin. This is because

1 The basic figure of eight retrieve. The angler has pinched the line and moves his hand round to grasp the loop.

2 The angler grips the loop. Notice the thumb and index finger of the rod hand guiding the line.

3 The angler moves his hand round again to pinch the line and repeat the process.

(1)

(2)

(3)

(1) (2) (3) (4) (5)

1 An advanced figure of eight retrieve which keeps the line in the hand. A loop is made around the index finger.

2 The line is taken round the back of the hand, then in front of the second finger and the index finger.

3 The line is then taken round the back of the index and second fingers then passed in front of the third and fourth fingers.

4 Take the line round the back of the hand, passing in front of the second and index fingers.

5 Continue the process until the line is retrieved. With practice it is possible to cast straight off the fingers.

the method is adaptable, and the water can be searched thoroughly to find the fish.

The nymphs generally used for this type of fishing are leaded. I always use the same amount of lead in each nymph, and control the depth by counting after the cast just as I would with a lure. The favourite nymphs are Pheasant Tail, Damsel Fly, May Fly, Shrimp, Stick Fly.

When fishing with leaded nymphs you can, in fact, get the best of

1 The stripping retrieve. The right hand traps the line against the rod. The left hand is ready to pull the line.

2 The right hand releases the line as the left hand pulls. The process is repeated.

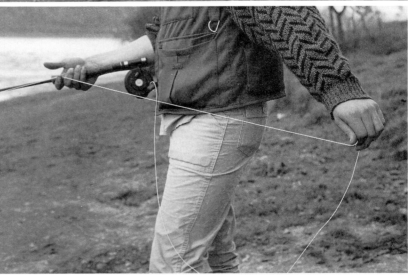

both worlds, as it is quite simple to drop a nymph into the path of a rising trout. However, it must be borne in mind that the nymph will create some disturbance as it hits the water, and it will obviously sink faster than an unleaded nymph. Your success rate in casting to rising trout with a leaded nymph may well be lower than when using an unleaded nymph, so it is advisable to change nymphs if the trout start rising in any numbers.

My approach to the water is exactly the same as I use when fishing a sub-surface nymph. It is even more important to keep your silhouette off the skyline, and to wear clothing that merges with the background. A trout's field of vision increases dramatically as it gets deeper.

It is still worth while searching the margins before casting any great distance, and be sure to retrieve in over the marginal shelf. Trout may treat the shelf as a boundary, and take a nymph to stop it 'getting away'.

With the leaded nymph you can search the water thoroughly for fish. I like to use as long a leader as I can comfortably manage, but rarely go over 20 feet. I count the same as when fishing a lure, but this is only practical when there is little or no surface drift. The point of the leader has a breaking strain of between 4 and 6 lb depending on conditions. On calm days when takes are easily visible I find 4 lb sufficient, but on windy days when there is a lot of surface water movement I increase to 6 lb just in case the trout take the faster-moving nymph harder.

A double-taper line is still the main weapon, but it is often necessary to go onto a weight-forward line in order to penetrate the wind or to gain extra distance. A 10-foot rod is my favourite, but this depends upon the type of water that I am fishing. However, avoid soft-action rods which take too long, and have insufficient power, to set the hook at a distance.

Make sure that the fly line is well greased, then stretch the leader and apply a sinking compound. Although the nymph might be leaded, the natural buoyancy of the new monofilament may well hold it up in the water.

There are two basic methods of presentation to trout feeding on deep nymphs.

Figure of eight

The method is as described on page 99. This is the standard retrieve when fishing leaded nymphs. It is infinitely variable, and keeps the angler in touch with the fly. As the line is always to hand, the angler's reaction to takes is very fast.

Stripping retrieve

Again, this is described on page 99. Not so popular, but nevertheless successful. This retrieve can be used to induce takes.

Drift-fishing techniques are not so effective with deep nymphs, but they have been known to work when the fish are rather shy.

The deep nymph is usually retrieved at a slightly faster speed than the sub-surface nymph as we are usually fishing larger patterns. However, it must be remembered that we are still imitating natural aquatic animals, and they move slowly. Just because we are fishing deeper it does not mean that we have to fish faster.

As I have mentioned before, the deep nymph permits the angler to search through as well as across the water. There is no risk of causing 'V' wakes as the nymph and leader will be under the water surface. We are now fishing imitations of nymphs which are feeding on or around the lake bed, in weedbeds, or nymphs which are beginning their ascent to the surface to hatch. It is therefore necessary to use the longest leader we can within reason in order to search as deep as possible. If we are not fishing around weed beds we must certainly fish across the lake bed because that is where the main source of trout food will be.

The nymphs will usually be leaded to help get them down quickly, and we must bear in mind that we will not be fishing in a straight line from rod tip to fly any more. There will be an angle between the fly line lying across the water surface, and the leader going down to the nymph. This means that vibrationary indications of a take will be longer in reaching the angler. It is important in deep-nymph fishing to keep in contact with the nymph at all times although in windy conditions this can be rather difficult. Another point to bear in mind is that although the nymphs are designed to fish deeper, there is no reason why a trout will not take them near the surface. The angler must stay alert whilst waiting for the nymph to sink, as it is quite likely that the nymph will be taken on the drop. If the angler is not paying attention he will feel a quick pull and nothing more, or may even be completely unaware of the trout's interest. Of the two situations I prefer the latter. Ignorance is bliss.

The sub-surface nymph

When fishing sub-surface nymphs we are usually using buzzers or sedge pupa. These life forms have little movement. They cling to the underside of the water surface, then break through the surface film to hatch. It is at this time that they are most vulnerable to attack by trout. Buzzers and caenis (Fisherman's Curse) can hatch in their thousands, and the trout become preoccupied. This can be a very difficult time for the angler for a number of reasons. The trout have such a tremendous choice of food that they may well be difficult to tempt. They may be feeding on one certain colour of buzzer to the exclusion of everything else. The hatch of fly might be so dense that the trout do not even notice your offering. Under these circumstances fishing techniques have to be tried and discarded until the successful method is found.

Static fishing

The static technique can be used on a still day in order to ascertain the size and colour of the nymphs that are hatching. It is an ideal method to use when fishing a team of nymphs. Most anglers prefer to fish a single nymph, but when fishing a hatch of fly that may only last for twenty minutes, it is important to find the successful pattern quickly.

The typical leader will be between 15 and 18 feet long. The point fly will be the heaviest, and the middle fly will be no closer than 4 feet from the point. The top dropper will be at least 4 feet above the middle dropper. Droppers should ideally be no longer than 3 inches, but if it might be necessary to change flies a few times during the session it is advisable to tie them about 5 inches long. This set-up keeps the nymphs well away from the fly line, and holds them just under the surface. Floatant is applied to the leader at regular intervals with a blob on each dropper knot.

The fishing technique is simplicity itself. Just a matter of casting delicately among the rising fish and waiting. Simple it might be, effective it can be, but exciting it is not.

Drift fishing

The drift technique can be used in the same way as the static method when a breeze is blowing virtually parallel to the bank. The same leader configuration is ideal. First it is necessary to find the rising fish, and to position yourself slightly downwind of them. Cast across and slightly upwind, then allow the nymphs to drift down to the fish. The presentation should be very good, as the nymphs will be travelling at the same speed as the food forms that the trout are feeding on.

If you can cast directly across the wind, the nymphs will almost immediately start to curve in towards the bank as a belly forms in the line. This can also prove an effective method, but it is necessary to keep directly in touch with the nymphs and not to let the belly of the line get too large.

Figure of eight

The figure of eight retrieve (see page 99) can be used under all conditions whether it be a flat calm or a strong breeze. It is the ideal retrieve to use when the water is flat as it can be slowed down in order to avoid 'V' wakes forming behind the leader knots. It is the retrieve I use when fishing across the wind, even when conditions get somewhat rough. Just because the water has a few waves on it, it does not mean that you cannot fish the nymph. In fact with the exception of casting, rougher weather is in the angler's favour. The fish's field of vision is impaired, the disturbance caused by the cast is lessened due to the natural disturbance of the water, sunlight is broken up by the wave action, and food forms can be washed out of their hideouts.

When fishing down and across a strong wind, it does not worry me unduly if the line forms a belly on the water, provided that I can keep in contact with the nymph. The retrieve speed is controlled by the speed of the surface water which will drift the nymphs down-wind and into the bank. The faster the surface-water speed, the slower the retrieve should be in order to keep the nymph fishing at a sensible speed. The fish, of course, will expect their food to arrive a little faster anyway.

Stripping retrieve

The stripping retrieve (see page 99) is a useful method of sub-surface fishing. It can be used to good effect to induce takes from nymphing trout. A pull of a couple of feet followed by a prolonged pause will cause the nymph to move up and forward, then sink slowly down. When a nymph is cast in front of a nymphing trout, a swift pull to bring the nymph across the trout's field of view can have spectacular results. Most takes will occur when the nymph is sinking, and it is imperative that the angler quickly regrips the line after the pull of the retrieve so that he is in the right position to react very quickly to the take. The stripping retrieve is the fastest retrieve that the angler will use, and it must be remembered that the fly line, and any leader lying on the surface, will cause 'V' wakes in the water. There is no doubt that these wakes do put trout off. I prefer to fish this method with an ungreased leader, and to cast to specific fish in order that I can start the retrieve almost immediately, before the nymph sinks too deep to be effective.

The take

There is nothing more exciting than watching trout head and tail upwind. You know that they are feeding near the surface, and everything is in your favour. All you have to do is to present the correct fly in the correct manner. Local knowledge is of great value. 'We get brown buzzers here,' or 'I always use a pheasant tail', and other similar comments are always gratefully accepted and stored away for reference at a future date.

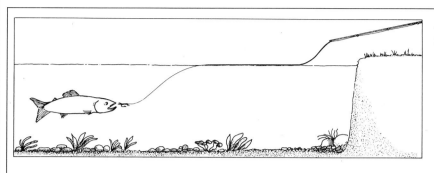

A typical take on the nymph.

1 Before the take. There is a loop of line between the rod and the water surface.

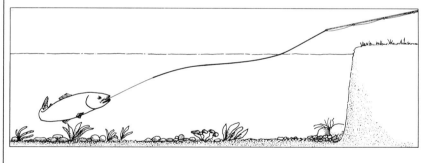

2 The take. The tip of the fly line is pulled under, and the loop straightens. STRIKE . . .

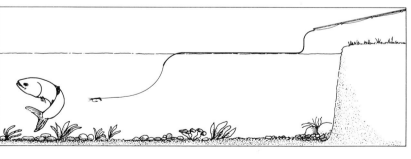

3 The pull. The trout starts to turn and you feel the take on your fingers. Strike now and you will get the fish if you are lucky.

4 Too late. The trout has ejected the nymph. All you have to show for it is a sunken tip to your fly line.

1 The rod top — water loop during a slow figure-
   of-eight retrieve.

2 The take.

3 The strike.

Sooner or later a trout will take your nymph, but will you realise it when it happens, or will you realise it too late and miss the best fish of the day?

Anglers newly recruited to stillwater trout fishing who start quite rightly with lures, have two basic conversion problems when taking up nymph fishing. One problem is the slowing down of their retrieve, but the major problem is one of concentration. Now I am the first to admit that fishing is a hobby which should be enjoyed, but how better to enjoy a hobby than to be successful at it? Concentration is the key to successful nymph fishing. When fishing a lure we rely on feeling the trout take. We use a comparatively fast retrieve, and the trout take the lure out of aggression, hunger or inquisitiveness. They have to chase and intercept the lure quickly, or as far as they are concerned they will miss it. The stripping retrieve automatically sets the hook on the next pull. The line is relatively straight and there is little delay in the take registering with the angler. Nymph fishing is different. The trout have plenty of time

The loop as seen from the angler's viewpoint.

to take the nymph, and take it just as they would a natural nymph. They know that it cannot escape because none have escaped them before. Therefore the take is leisurely, slow and deliberate. The rate of retrieve is not fast enough to set the hook automatically, and should the angler feel a pull on the line, it is probably after the trout has discovered that it has been deceived and has taken fright. I wonder just how many times a trout has taken my nymph and rejected it without me realising it. I do know that it happens regularly judging from the number of takes I see in various ways, but am not fast enough to react to successfully. It is necessary therefore to learn to recognise the signs of a trout taking your nymph. When fishing sub-surface it is possible to see the take, especially when the trout head and tails at your nymph. You may even see the flash of the fish as it turns on taking the nymph. In either case you can tighten into the fish. This is the essence of good nymph fishing — speed to strike the trout when it takes the nymph.

The main requirement then is to be able to see and recognise takes. Your selection of tackle can help you here. The farther that you can see along your fly line, the sooner you will see signs of a take. Your fly line for example can be of a bright colour such as yellow, pink or orange. I have yet to be convinced that a bright fly line used in conjunction with a long leader disturbs fish because of its colour. If you do not like this idea, Cortland manufacture a nymph tip taper which is a standard weight-forward line coloured their usual pink, but with a fluorescent tip section to which the leader is attached.

Striker tabs are small strips of self-adhesive fluorescent material which are folded round the butt of the leader. They are made of close cellular sponge material and are buoyant. Red fluorescent wool (about four strands, each 3 inches long) can be soaked in floatant and tied to the end of the fly line. It causes little resistance, but certainly helps with detection. All of these methods help the angler to detect takes long before they register on the rod top as he has something to look at, just like a coarse angler watches a float. They all work well in calm water, but tend to lose their efficiency in rough weather.

This still leaves the angler with the problem of how to detect takes when the weather is not perfect and, let's face it, in this country the weather is very rarely perfect. The easiest way to describe the best method is to work through a full retrieve.

Let us imagine that we have searched the margins around our chosen pitch, and have now decided to try further out. There are one or two fish rising spasmodically, but nothing to get excited about, and we will have to fish the water.

Hopefully the cast is a good one, and our nymph lands fairly delicately about 25 yards out with the leader fully extended. A quick pull on the line gets everything straight, and we watch the end of the fly line while the nymph sinks for a few seconds. We look for the tip of the line to be pulled down, preferably to either right or left as it is easier to see. Nothing happens. The water surface is rippled and sunlight is reflecting towards us. Even with Polaroid glasses we cannot comfortably see the end of the line. To avoid eye strain, a blinding headache, and tiredness we do not try to look at the end of the fly line. We lift the rod tip so that it is about 2 feet off the water, and start our figure-of-eight retrieve. A loop of line extends from the rod top to the water in a gentle curve, the shape of the curve being governed by the speed of the surface-water drift and by the speed of our retrieve. We continue the retrieve and watch the loop of line. If it rises it means that the line has tightened, there is a resistance. That resistance can only be caused by the nymph stopping whilst we are still retrieving. Only three things can cause this; the bottom, weed, or a fish. If that loop of line rises – STRIKE!

Let us suppose that nothing happens and the tip of the fly is now coming into view, perhaps 10 yards out. We now revert to watching the tip of the line. It may move right or left, or gently submerge – STRIKE!

If we are fishing an area with a narrow marginal shelf continue retrieving then lift the rod slowly and let the leader come out of the water. You are making the nymph rise. This change of direction can induce a take. If it does, you will feel it directly on the rod top. No chance to strike this time; the fish is either on, or headed in the opposite direction at some speed.

The foregoing routine is the best that I have found for nymph fishing, and is used by many successful nymph fishermen around the country. Exactly the same method can be used when fishing from a boat. The basic idea is that you strike the fish before the fish strikes you.

In very windy weather when the water is rough, any method utilising a floating line becomes more difficult. However, all is not lost. The surface-water drift increases the speed of the nymph. The wave action hides any disturbance that casting might create, and also limits the trout's field of vision. The trout are not so wary, and take the nymphs more firmly. The basic rules still apply but, to be honest, you have more chance of taking fish that pull the line or bounce the rod top because the takes are firmer. When all is said and done however, you will catch more trout if you hook them, rather than relying on them to hook themselves.

Chapter 11

Nymph fishing with sinking lines

There comes a time sometime every season when everything seems to be against the angler. There is a howling gale blowing down the reservoir, but it is June and the water is full of food forms. The trout are preoccupied with nymphs; there are so many of them about that feeding is easy, and they cannot be bothered to chase a lure.

The poor angler has tried a floating line with leaded nymphs, but it has drifted into the side so quickly that it was a waste of time. The nymph must have been travelling at the same speed as a lure, and no self-respecting trout would look at it. The angler resorts to a lure; at least the line is not affected by the surface drift, and he can fish a decent retrieve but, in all honesty, he does not hold out much hope.

All is not lost, however. You can effectively fish a nymph on a sinking line, not only because the weather is rough, but also when there is bright sunshine which has forced the fish to go deeper.

I well remember a trip to Upper Tamar Lake in late summer 1983 with Les Tanner, my regular fishing partner. We had booked a boat, but when we arrived a gale was blowing down the reservoir towards the dam. We tried to row the boat, but after ten minutes we gave up having made no headway at all. The reservoir was low, and we squelched down the bank through the mud and eventually started fishing. During the morning Les had one fish, and I missed a couple. At lunch time we squelched back up to the office for a cup of tea, but the weather was so bad that Shirley, the wife of warden Ken Spalding, had not bothered to open their delightful little shop. To cap it all, I had stumbled into a horrible little muddy ditch, and did not smell too good. Perhaps that is why Shirley did not open the shop.

Les and I decided to fish the area on the opposite bank in the hope that we could cross the stream that goes into the arm, and fish with the wind in the afternoon. No such luck; the mud stopped us. We had no choice but to fish the arm almost into the wind.

This was the first time that I used a nymph on a sinking line. I was testing a Cortland weight-forward Intermediate which has a sink rate of about one inch per second, and selected a brown chenille nymph which was working wonders at Kennick, my local reservoir. To be honest, I was just going through the motions when I felt a pull, nothing more. I started fishing more seriously and caught a fish. Les put up his Cortland Slow Sinker and used an identical nymph. To cut the story short, in an hour and a half we landed nine trout and missed a few more. The result: a limit each on a day when any sane person would have stayed at home.

A sunny day at Wimbleball during 1985 (yes, we had one) also comes to mind. The result, a double limit on a damsel nymph using the same Cortland Intermediate. My nymph was similar to many others being used (in fact I handed some of mine out to friends) but I caught the majority of the fish.

Since that trip in 1983 Les and I have refined our methods of nymph fishing with sinking lines, and we now willingly change from floating to sunk-line fishing with nymphs because we have confidence in the method. Confidence plays a large part in angling.

The first thing to make clear is that we do not use sink-tip lines. They are difficult to cast, do not offer good presentation, are susceptible to surface-water drift, and form an additional angle in

The angler holds his rod at right angles to the line when nymph fishing with an intermediate line.

the line from the nymph to the rod top. Our lines are either weight-forward or double-taper intermediates or slow sinkers. The leader is 12 to 15 feet long, with a 4 to 6 lb point. A knotless, tapered leader is preferred, and at no time do we use droppers.

Our rods are 10-foot AFTM 7–8 models with a very positive middle-to-tip action.

Our nymphs are the standard deep water patterns such as Damsel Nymph, Pheasant Tail Nymph, Mayfly Nymph, Stick Fly, which we tie both leaded and unleaded. The unleaded nymphs are used to fish near the surface, and the leaded nymphs permit us to fish much deeper than is possible with a floating line and long leader.

Near-surface fishing

This method is used mainly on dull, windy days purely to avoid the surface-water drift. The unleaded nymphs are used to maintain as much height in the water as possible.

After the cast is made, the retrieve is started immediately. The line will form a slight belly, but as it sinks below the level of the water being affected by the surface-water drift it will straighten as the line is retrieved. A figure-of-eight retrieve is used, slightly faster than that used with a floating line. Immediately after the cast a loop of line will form from the rod tip to the water surface, and it is most important to watch this just as we do when using a floating line. However, as the line sinks, the drag increases and the loop tends to straighten out. This obviously makes the detection of takes more difficult, but a change of stance can help considerably. Instead of pointing the rod towards the line, we turn 90 degrees so that the rod points along the bank. If the wind is blowing along the bank it makes fishing easier if you turn your back to the wind. The line from rod tip to water is now in full view. We can see the exact angle of the loop, and can strike if it changes. Obviously the loop is not so pronounced and detection of takes is slightly more difficult, but the change of stance helps us in another way. We use the tip of the rod as a bite indicator, much like the quiver tips that coarse anglers use. The sideways stance also helps us to strike more quickly, taking the rod through a larger arc than is possible with a vertical strike.

Deep-water fishing

Nymphs, as we know, spend most of their time on or around the bottom of the lakes, so it makes sense to fish nymph imitations deep as that is where the trout expect to find them.

However, we restrict ourselves to intermediate and slow-sinking lines, but use the leaded nymphs to attain the required depth. The faster-sinking lines can cause problems especially if the lake bed is littered with rocks or weed, as they will pull the nymph into underwater hazards whereas the less dense lines will ride more easily above any underwater obstruction. It is also beneficial to use a nymph that sinks at a faster rate than the fly line as this helps to keep a straight line between nymph and rod tip. If the lake bed is particularly snaggy, it may be necessary to revert to unleaded nymphs in an attempt to avoid undue loss of flies.

The tackle used is exactly the same as for near-surface fishing, but we may lean towards a slightly heavier point, perhaps 5 or 6 lb, in case we have to pull the nymph out of underwater obstructions. Do remember if the nymph gets snagged to check the point before recasting. It is very annoying to get plenty of takes and fail to hook any of them only to find that the hook point has broken off at the barb.

The cast is made, and the count starts just as in lure fishing. If the tackle is well balanced, the leaded nymph will pull the leader then the fly line under the water. This results in the fly line submerging tip first and gradually submerging progressively along its length towards you. At this time there will be a loop of line between the rod top and the water which you can use for bite detection, but if possible watch the point where the fly line is submerging. That point will move towards you at a steady rate. If it speeds up – STRIKE, and if it stops – STRIKE. Many trout can be taken on the drop using this method. Once the selected depth has been attained, the retrieve is the figure of eight. The stance is at right angles to the line so that the rod-tip-to-water loop can be seen clearly.

There are two typical takes when using this method. The sudden pull is most common, but both Les and I have struck instinctively at a tightening-up sensation when it appears that the trout has taken the nymph and not moved.

When nymph fishing with leaded nymphs on either floating or sinking lines there will come a time when you will strike into a fish and land it. Then you will think back and wonder, 'Why did I strike then?' This is the wonderful sixth sense that many anglers experience yet none can explain. It comes with experience and confidence. Personally I am very grateful for its presence.

Chapter 12

Flies for the season

It is a sad fact that more flies catch anglers than catch fish. This is even more so in tackle shops where in a number of cases flies imported from the Far East or Africa bear little or no resemblance to the pattern as it was originally designed. The angler who does not tie his own flies can therefore be put at a disadvantage by having to rely on flies tied by someone who has never studied fly patterns, and has never seen a trout.

Having said that, it must be made clear that the vast majority of tackle shops stock reasonable-quality flies, so it is up to the angler to learn to distinguish between quality and rubbish. Even if you do not tie your own flies, it is worth your time to learn to identify various feathers, colours, and most importantly fly patterns in order to ensure that you have a comprehensive selection in your fly box.

We all carry the odd patterns that we have purchased or tied with no real idea of when we shall use them. These are useful standbys which we can employ when we are at our wits' end on one of those hopefully not too common days, usually in July and August, when the trout do not seem particularly hungry.

In this chapter I plan to give you a basic list of flies, nymphs, and lures which are generally accepted to be of use on the majority of stillwater fisheries. Every fishery has its own flies which work better than others, some of which will not be listed here as they may be only of local interest. But generally speaking, an angler with a selection of the following patterns will find something in his box that will work.

Lures

The most popular colours for lures are black, white, orange, and green. Pink and blue lures have been in fashion recently, but I am not sure that their success has been proved.

Baby Doll

Designed by Brian Kench

Hook	8–10 Longshank
Silk	Black

Tail	White baby wool
Back	White baby wool
Body	White baby wool
Head	Black tying silk

Useful in all conditions, but throw it away as soon as the wool gets dirty. Can be used greased-up as a static fry imitation in the autumn.

ADAPTATIONS: Undertaker as above, but in black, with a silver-lurex rib.

OTHER USEFUL COLOURS: Orange, green

Designed by Bob Church   **Appetiser**

Hook	6–8 Longshank
Silk	Black
Tail	Green and red cock hackle fibres
Rib	Silver tinsel
Body	White chenille
Hackle (False)	Green and red cock hackle plus grey mallard

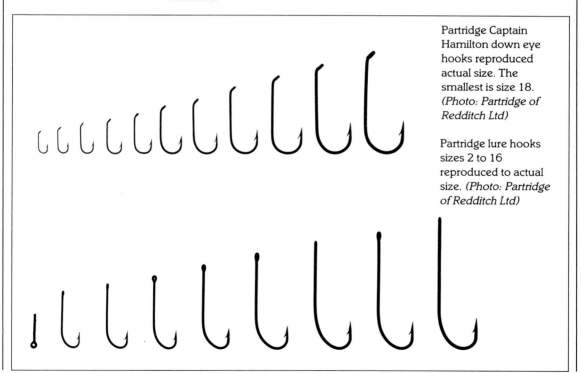

Partridge Captain Hamilton down eye hooks reproduced actual size. The smallest is size 18. *(Photo: Partridge of Redditch Ltd)*

Partridge lure hooks sizes 2 to 16 reproduced to actual size. *(Photo: Partridge of Redditch Ltd)*

Wing	White marabou with grey squirrel over

Useful throughout the season, especially in the autumn for fry feeders. Can be tied as a tandem lure for deep fishing.

Viva

Designed by Victor Furse

Hook	6–8 Longshank
Silk	Black
Tail	DFM green wool
Rib	Wide silver tinsel
Body	Black chenille
Wing	Mixture of black marabou and goathair

One of the classic lures. Useful throughout the season, especially during the first two months.
ADAPTATIONS: Replace goathair with a generous portion of black marabou. Tie in green DFM chenille butt to replace tag.
OTHER USEFUL COLOURS: White Viva

Sweeney Todd

Designed by the late Dick Walker

Hook	6–10 Longshank
Silk	Black
Rib	Silver tinsel
Body	Black floss
Collar	DFM magenta floss
Hackle (false)	Red cock hackle
Wing	Black squirrel tail

Another of the classic lures designed by an undoubted master. Will take fish at any depth, but especially useful just under the surface.

Whiskey Fly

Designed by Albert Whillock

Hook	6–8 Longshank
Silk	Scarlet fluorescent nylon floss
Body	Varnished gold or silver Sellotape
Tag	DRF scarlet nylon floss
Rib	DRF scarlet nylon floss
Hackle	Hot orange cock hackle
Wing	Hot orange calf tail
Head	DRF scarlet nylon floss

A lure that in the early 1970s set people thinking about alternative colours. Fishes well just under the surface on hot sunny days, and is also useful when the water is green with suspended algae.
ADAPTATIONS: Substitute Sellotape with gold or silver lurex. Use marabou in place of calf tail.

Adapted from a New Zealand pattern by Dick Shrive   **Missionary**

Hook	6–10 Longshank
Silk	Black
Tail	Scarlet cock hackle fibres
Throat hackle	Scarlet cock hackle fibres
Body	White chenille
Rib	Silver tinsel
Wing	Grey mallard feather tied in flat

Another famous lure from one of our top anglers. Undoubtedly a good fry imitation.
ADAPTATIONS: Substitute barred teal fibres for grey mallard to make a slimmer wing. This lets the lure sink faster, and it can be used with a faster retrieve.
OTHER USEFUL COLOURS: Yellow Missionary

Widely known as Dog Nobblers, and introduced to this country by **Leadheads**
Trevor Housby. Adapted from American patterns.

Hook	6–10 Longshank
Silk	Black
Tail	Generous bunch of marabou
Body	Chenille
Rib	Silver tinsel
Hackle	Large cock hackle
Head	Split shot crimped onto hook shank
	Painted black with yellow/black eyes if required

You will notice that I have not mentioned colours. Almost anything goes, including lure derivatives: Black – Viva; White – Jack Frost; Orange, pink, blue, brown, green. Designed to fish in an undulating manner due to the split shot pinched on just behind the eye of the hook. Suitable for fishing on floating or sinking lines, but watch out when you are casting. They do tend to fly low.

ADAPTATIONS: Due to the recent increase in fashion consciousness by anglers, many adaptations of these lures have been designed. We hear such names as Frog Nobblers, Poodles, Nasties . . .

Add a few fibres of Flashabou or Lureflash to the tail for some added sparkle.

Muddlers

Designed by Don Gapen in the USA and introduced to the UK by Tom Saville of Nottingham

Hook	6–10 Longshank
Silk	Brown
Tail	Oak turkey
Body	Gold lurex
Rib	Oval gold tinsel
Wing	Grey squirrel flanked with oak turkey
Head	Natural deer hair spun and clipped

Probably the most famous of all lures, and one that catches fish consistently throughout the season. The buoyant deer-hair head keeps the lure off the bottom, so that it can be fished at all depths. Towards the end of the season, a muddler stripped across the waves can induce ferocious takes from trout which will follow it for yards.

ADAPTATIONS: Muddlers tied on standard shank hooks fish well during sedge hatches, and are even used for loch-style fishing.

OTHER USEFUL COLOURS: Substitute tail, body, and winging materials with materials of the following colours: black, white, orange, yellow.

Ace of Spades

Designed by David Collyer

Hook	6–12 Longshank
Silk	Black
Rib	Silver tinsel
Body	Black chenille
Wing	Black hen hackle tied matuka style
Overwing	Bronze mallard – dark
Hackle	Guinea fowl

Another slow-sinking lure designed to produce a very solid silhouette. Can be fished at all depths, but works well when retrieved slowly along the bottom.

ADAPTATIONS: A lead wire under the body can be incorporated to help fish deep water, but this can be more of a hindrance than a help.

Designed by Bob Church   **Church Fry**

Hook	4–10 Longshank
Rib	Silver lurex
Body	Orange floss silk
Collar	DFM magenta floss
Hackle	Orange cock hackle fibres
Wing	Grey squirrel tail

A useful fly for fishing deep as it shows up well. Can be used effectively as a fry imitation.
ADAPTATIONS: Use orange chenille for the body in place of floss silk. Try a white bearded hackle instead of orange.

Due to the multitude of nymphs found in our still waters, it is   **Nymphs** necessary to tie a fair selection of sizes and colours in order to cover most eventualities.

Designed by the late Dick Walker   **Buzzer Pupa**

Hook	10–18 Down eye
Silk	Black
Breathing tubes	White cock hackle fibres
Rib	Silver wire
Body	Tying silk or floss
Thorax	Peacock herl

Probably the most popular nymph, and certainly the most commonly found food in trout stomachs. Various colours are used.
ADAPTATIONS: Use white DFM fibres in place of white cock hackle.
USEFUL COLOURS: Black, green, red, orange, brown.

Designed by the late Dick Walker   **Pheasant Tail Nymph**

Hook	10–12 Down eye
Silk	Brown
Tail	Cock pheasant centre tail fibres
Rib	Copper wire
Body	As for tail
Thorax	As for tail
Wing cases	As for tail
Legs	As for tail

One of the best general nymph patterns ever designed. I fished the Upper Tamar Reservoir in Cornwall from its opening in 1976 to 1984 without a blank day, and this fly took more fish for me than any other. It works well on virtually all waters.

ADAPTATIONS: Use grey partridge hackle for the legs. Works well on a 12 long shank hook to imitate larger nymphs. Can be used with a leaded underbody to fish deeper.

OTHER USEFUL COLOURS: Various colours of seal's fur can be used for the thorax, e.g. black, green, orange, cream.

Damsel Nymph

Designed by Geoff Hirst

Hook	10–12 Longshank
Silk	Olive green
Tail	Cock pheasant centre tail fibres
Rib	Gold wire
Body	Dark olive green mohair
Thorax	Rabbit fur
Wing cases	Cock pheasant centre tail fibres
Legs	Grey partridge hackle fibres

Geoff designed this nymph primarily for use at Kennick Reservoir in Devon, but it has proved its worth on many waters around the country.

ADAPTATIONS: Use a lead wire underbody to fish greater depths. Substitute rabbit fur with olive mohair or seal's fur of various colours.

Corixa

Designed by John Mitchell

Hook	10–12 Down eye
Silk	Brown
Body	White chenille
Rib	Silver wire
Wing case	Cock pheasant centre tail fibres (varnished)
Paddles	Two cock pheasant centre tail fibres

I used this pattern initially at Bewl Bridge, but since then have found that it works well on most waters where corixae are present. It can be fished on a floating or slow-sinking line.

ADAPTATIONS: A lead underbody can be incorporated in order to allow the angler to fish 'sink and draw' on a floating line.

Designed by John Goddard **Sedge Pupa**

Hook	10–12 Longshank
Silk	Brown
Body	Seal's fur
Rib	Silver lurex or oval tinsel
Thorax	Condor herl (dark brown) or dyed turkey
Wing cases	Three pale-coloured feather fibres doubled and redoubled
Hackle	Rusty hen hackle tied sparsely

A selection of colours on both size 10 and 12 hooks should be sufficient to deal with most sedge rises. Bear in mind that there are many different species of sedge, and it may be necessary to tie a pattern for a particular water.
USEFUL COLOURS: The body material of seal's fur can be cream, brown, orange, green.

Designed by the late Dick Walker **Shrimp**

Hook	10–12 Down eye
Silk	Brown
Body	Olive wool over layers of lead-foil bound on to the back of the hook shank
Hackle	Ginger cock hackle palmered the length of the body, and clipped off the sides and back
Back	Soaked in varnish to produce hard, smooth back

An excellent pattern for waters containing shrimp. This fly will swim upside down and is very useful for fishing near the bottom without getting snagged.
ADAPTATIONS: Use olive raffeine over the back (well varnished) to produce a more shell-like appearance.
OTHER USEFUL COLOURS: Use dull orange wool in the spring to represent mating colour.

Designed by Arthur Cove **Cove's Pheasant Tail Nymph**

Hook	8–12 Longshank
Silk	Brown
Rib	Copper wire
Body	Cock pheasant centre tail fibres
Thorax	Blue rabbit under-fur

Designed to sink quickly. Usually used on a long leader of 20 feet or so. This nymph acts as an anchor on the point when fishing a team of flies. It has accounted for some very large fish.

ADAPTATIONS: Obviously a nymph that can be tied with various coloured thorax. It can be leaded in the smaller sizes.

Stick Fly

Designed by David Collyer

Hook	8–10 Longshank
Silk	Black
Rib	Copper, silver or gold wire
Body	Cock pheasant centre tail fibres
Thorax	Yellow or off-white floss
Hackle	Pale ginger cock hackle
Head	Gold with tying silk heavily varnished

Designed to imitate the larval form of the sedge flies which build a camouflaged case around themselves. A fly that whilst usually fished on or near the bottom has taken its fair share of fish just under the surface.

ADAPTATIONS: The body can be leaded if required.

OTHER USEFUL COLOURS: The body material can be substituted with dubbed seal's fur, dyed swan feathers or peacock herl of various colours to imitate the colour prevalent in the particular water being fished. A DFM yellow tag seems to enhance the fish-catching qualities of this fly.

Mayfly Nymph

Designed by Taff Price

Hook	10 Longshank
Silk	Brown
Tail	Cock pheasant centre tail fibres (3)
Body	Cream nylon wool
Rib	Brown ostrich herl with two turns of herl just behind the thorax
Wing case	Cock pheasant centre tail fibres
Thorax	Cream wool
Legs	Cock pheasant centre tail fibres turned down from wing case

A nymph that has proved effective on many waters, some of which do not have a natural mayfly population.

ADAPTATIONS: A lead underbody can be added for fishing deep.

Designed by Tom Ivens **Ivens' Brown and Green Nymph**

Hook	6–10 Down eye
Silk	Olive or brown
Tail	Four strands of peacock herl
Rib	Oval gold tinsel or wire
Body	Brown and green ostrich herl (one strand of each)
Back	Four strands of green peacock herl
Head	Peacock herl

A very successful nymph pattern, best fished just under the surface. It can be used equally with slow or fast figure-of-eight retrieves.
ADAPTATIONS: A lead underbody can be incorporated for fishing deep, but it is best to keep the lead to a minimum.

Anglers seem to associate wet flies with loch-style fishing, but a number of them serve very well from the bank, and it is worth having a selection with you. **Wet flies**

Designed by Tom Ivens **Black and Peacock Spider**

Hook	6–12 Down eye
Body	Bronze peacock herl wound over wet varnish
Hackle	Dyed black hen hackle

If you go to fly-tying lessons this will probably be the first fly that you will ever tie. To my mind it goes to prove that the simplest patterns can be the most productive. The B & P, as it is commonly known, catches fish everywhere.
ADAPTATIONS : Add a lead underbody if required. Add a floss underbody to make a bulkier pattern. Use black cock hackles to enhance floating qualities if required.

Designed by James Ogden **Invicta**

Hook	10–14 Down eye
Silk	Brown
Tail	Golden pheasant crest feathers
Rib	Oval gold tinsel
Body	Yellow seal's fur
Body hackle	Red game cock palmered sparsely

| Throat hackle | Blue jay |
| Wing | Hen pheasant centre tail |

No-one knows exactly what this fly represents, but the general opinion is that it is a good imitation of a hatching sedge. It is best fished just under the surface in July, August and September.

ADAPTATIONS: Silver Invicta: substitute flat silver tinsel or lurex for yellow seal's fur. Red Tailed Invicta: substitute scarlet ibis for golden pheasant crest feathers.

Mallard and Claret   Attributed to William Murdoch

Hook	8–14 Down eye
Silk	Claret
Tail	Golden pheasant tippet fibres
Rib	Fine gold wire
Body	Claret seal's fur
Hackle	Claret or red cock
Wing	Bronze mallard

A fly which, although many years old, has gained popularity rapidly during the last few years. It can work wonders during hatches of black or dark red buzzers.

ADAPTATIONS: Claret wool can be used in place of seal's fur.

Peter Ross   Designed by Peter Ross

Hook	8–14 Down eye
Silk	Black
Tail	Golden pheasant tippet fibres
Body	Rear half – flat silver lurex
	Front half – red seal's fur
Rib	Fine oval silver tinsel
Hackle	Black hen
Wing	Barred teal feathers

Often thought to imitate fry, and fished fairly quickly just under the surface from July onwards. Usually fished singly, or on the point of a team.

Greenwell's Glory   Designed for Canon William Greenwell

| Hook | 12–14 Down eye |
| Silk | Waxed primrose |

Body	Waxed primrose tying silk
Rib	Gold wire
Hackle	Furnace cock
Wing	Starling or blackbird primary

The wet version of the fly which is probably better known than any other. Thought to represent nymphs of olives, this fly can be fished on floating or slow-sinking lines throughout the summer. Slow- to medium-speed retrieves appear to get the best results.

Designed by Doctor Bell   **The Grenadier**

Hook	12–14 Down eye
Body	Hot orange seal's fur
Rib	Oval gold tinsel or wire
Hackle	Sparse furnace cock

Regarded by many as the best bob fly from July onwards when the sedge are hatching. Designed for use at Blagdon, but has proved itself on many waters from both boat and bank.
ADAPTATIONS: Use hot orange wool in place of seal's fur.

Designer unknown   **Zulu**

Hook	10–14 Down eye
Silk	Black
Tail	Scarlet wool cut short
Rib	Fine flat silver lurex
Body	Black seal's fur or wool
Hackle	Black cock – palmered

A very old fly that constantly produces fish particularly when fished as a bob fly on a team of three. A good general pattern all season through.

Derived from the salmon fly of the same name   **Dunkeld**

Hook	8–12 Down eye
Silk	Black
Tail	Golden pheasant crest
Ribbing	Fine gold wire (optional)
Body	Flat gold lurex
Hackle	Hot orange cock

Wing	Bronze mallard
Cheeks	Jungle cock eye

Originally a salmon-fly, the Dunkeld has been adapted for either sea-trout or lake-trout fishing. Usually fished singly, or on the point of a team, this is an attractor pattern generally believed to imitate a small fish.

ADAPTATIONS: The hot orange hackle can be tied either as a throat hackle or palmered down the body and secured by the wire rib.

Connemara Black

Possibly of Irish origin

Hook	8–14 Down eye
Silk	Black
Tail	Golden pheasant crest
Rib	Oval silver tinsel or wire
Body	Black seal's fur
Hackle	Blue jay and black cock
Wing	Bronze mallard

A regular standby pattern which can be fished at all depths throughout the season. The dark silhouette makes it a good evening fly.

Wickham's Fancy

Designed by T. C. Wickham

Hook	10–16 Down eye
Silk	Yellow
Tail	Red game cock fibres
Rib	Gold wire
Body	Flat gold lurex
Body hackle	Palmered red game cock
Throat hackle	Red game cock
Wing	Starling primary feather

Not a truly imitative pattern, the Wickham's is a useful general-purpose fly which can be fished individually, or as part of a team. Appears to do better when fished on a slow-sinking line.

Dry flies

Sometimes ignored by stillwater anglers, there is no doubt that the dry fly has its place in our fly boxes. The use of a dry fly is an interesting diversion from the more usual methods, which at times really comes into its own.

Designed for Canon William Greenwell   **Greenwell's Glory**

Hook	12–16 Up eye
Silk	Waxed yellow silk
Rib	Gold wire
Body	Waxed yellow silk
Wing	Starling primary feather
Hackle	Furnace cock

An ideal imitation of either the lake olive or pond olive. These flies hatch at any time of the day from June onwards.

Designed by David Collyer   **Black Gnat**

Hook	16–18 Up eye
Silk	Black
Body	Dyed black swan or goose
Wing	Pale ginger cock hackle fibres
Hackle	Dyed black cock, very small

A good pattern throughout the season, not only when gnats abound, but at any time when small black flies are on the water.

A good rainbow taken on a dry Wickham's Fancy.

Daddy Long-legs   Designed by Andy Unwin

Hook	10 Up eye
Silk	Brown
Body	Deer-hair fibres whipped and varnished (detached)
Legs	Eight cock pheasant centre tail fibres, knotted twice
Wings	Brown cock hackle points
Hackle	Ginger cock

Come September, you must have one or two of these in your box. Once the trout get a taste for daddies they will ignore anything else whilst the supply lasts. Best fished with no movement at all, and cast with the wind to the edge of the ripple.

Walker's Sedge   Designed by the late Dick Walker

Hook	10–12 Up eye
Silk	Brown
Tag	Fluorescent orange wool
Body	Cock pheasant centre tail
Wings	Bunch of red cock hackles trimmed square
Hackle	Two red cock hackles

An evening fly for July, August, and September when the sedges are about. Best fished with a steady retrieve to cause a wake which will attract the trout.

Hawthorn Fly   Designer unknown

Hook	10–12 Up eye
Silk	Black
Body	Peacock herl
Hackle	Black cock
Head	One strand of peacock herl
Legs	Two dyed black swan feather fibres

The Hawthorn fly is a terrestrial which abounds in April and May. During a strong wind these flies are blown on to the water, and the trout love them. Fish the artificial with the wind, either static or with a slow retrieve.

American pattern   **Brown Bivisible**

Hook	10–12 Up eye
Silk	Brown
Tail	Tips of hackle
Body	Hackles
Hackles	Two brown cock hackles with one white hackle tied in front

A highly visible dry fly for use in poor light, or when there is a good wave. Works well when there are sedges about.
ADAPTATIONS: Black Bivisible: use black silk and black hackles instead of brown.

Designer unknown   **Coachman**

Hook	10–14 Up eye
Silk	Brown
Body	Bronze peacock herl
Wings	White cock hackle points
Hackle	Ginger cock

A very popular dry fly which can work well all through the season, especially when there are olives about.

Presumed to be a Welsh fly   **Coch-y-Bondhu**

Hook	8–14 Up eye
Silk	Black
Body	Bronze peacock herl
Hackle	Coch-y-bondhu or furnace

A useful fly throughout the season, but especially useful in June when beetles get blown on to the water. Can be fished sub-surface as well as dry.

Another Welsh pattern   **Grey Duster**

Hook	12–18 Up eye
Silk	Black
Body	Grey rabbit fur
Hackle	Badger cock

In its smaller sizes this fly is the nearest you can get to imitating caenis (fisherman's curse) which hatch by the thousand on still, warm evenings throughout July and August. Even then, there is no guarantee that you will be successful, but this fly is a useful pattern for smaller flies.

The foregoing then is a list of patterns which work well on most waters throughout the country. Your fly box will contain designs other than those listed; and conversely it will not contain all of the flies mentioned here. I cannot stress often enough the value of local knowledge regarding successful patterns on particular waters. If you cannot gain that knowledge, be methodical and work through your selection of flies at various depths and at various rates of retrieve. There are few days when the trout will not feed at all. It is a matter of finding them and also of finding what they are feeding on, then presenting your imitation correctly.

Chapter 13

Fighting fish

It is one thing to hook a trout, but another thing to successfully land it. Many fish are lost because the angler has made mistakes during the fight.

Earlier I said that tackle should be balanced according to the type of fishing being undertaken, but it must also be balanced to the fish that you are trying to catch.

A light leader of 2 lb breaking strain used for trout in snaggy water will mean lost fish. There is nothing to be proud of in leaving hooks in fish. We can all tell the stories of the one that got away, and we all lose fish from time to time, but there is something drastically wrong if an angler is continually broken while fighting fish.

Conversely, a heavy leader of perhaps 8 lb breaking strain used for small trout in open water will permit the angler to haul a fish ashore without it having the chance to put up a fight. There is also a chance that the force applied through such a heavy leader will break small hooks or pull the fly from the trout's mouth.

Therefore the balance between the breaking strain of the leader, the size of the fly and the conditions in which you are fishing is of paramount importance.

There are two ways of fighting fish in still water, either on the reel, or by hand.

Fighting on the reel

This is the purist method of fighting a fish, and is undoubtedly the best technique to use when fishing rivers and streams.

Initially it is necessary to reel in all the line that has already been retrieved whilst clamping it against the rod with the rod hand. This permits the fish to bounce about on the end without being brought under proper control. Once the line has been retrieved the fight proper can begin. An immediate advantage to this method is that no loose line gets under the angler's feet or tangles in undergrowth. Consequently, if line has to be given in a hurry, provided that the clutch on the reel is set correctly there are no problems.

However, there *are* disadvantages. Firstly, the amount of time it takes to reel up all the line which could be better spent in fighting the fish. Secondly, unless the reel is of the multiplier type such as the Gearfly there is a chance that should the trout run towards you, you may not be able to keep up which will result in loose line. Thirdly, the fact that both hands on the rod causes a decided lack of feel compared to the single-handed method.

Fighting by hand   This is the usual stillwater method of fighting fish. It is merely an extension of the stripping retrieve. As soon as the fish is hooked, the rod is raised and the angler is into the fight. Line already retrieved or gained in the fight is dropped to the ground.

The line is held against the handle of the rod by the index finger of the rod hand, whilst the retrieving hand either gains or gives line depending on what the fish is doing. Should the fish make a good run, the speed of the line is controlled by the retrieving hand, not by the rod hand.

The main disadvantages to this method are that loose line can get tangled in undergrowth or around the angler's feet, and that the angler must judge how much check to put on a running fish as he is unable to use the clutch on the reel. Having said that, it certainly appears that fish fought by hand arrive at the net more quickly than those fought off the reel.

Now, having stated the two options let us consider the actual fight regardless of which method you may use.

It is true to say that we never know exactly what a fish is going to do. We can guess that a fish hooked in shallow water will jump, whereas a fish hooked deep on a sinking line will not be seen for a while.

The first priority is to gain control. Whether a floating or sinking line is being used makes little difference except that a much larger bow will occur when using a sinking line. The first few times that I hooked a trout on a sinking line I was surprised to see my line entering the water in one direction whilst the fish surfaced somewhere else. This bow is obviously caused by the pressure of water on the line, and until the line has been properly tightened you do not have control. Raise the rod to about the eleven o'clock position to lift the line out of the water, then quickly retrieve line until you feel the actual movements of the fish. Now you are in control, the line is tight and you can tell what the fish is doing. You have a few seconds to guess the weight of the fish; this comes with practice and dictates just how you will handle the fight. Is it a stock fish or something bigger? Your judgement will usually be about right.

Keep the rod up at eleven o'clock for two reasons. Initially it helps to keep a tight line, and keeps as much line as possible out of the water. Secondly, it acts as a shock absorber, cushioning the line against the lunges of the fish. In fact your rod will fight the fish for you.

Do not be in too much of a hurry to bring the fish to the bank or boat. If you are bank fishing, there is nothing worse than having a lively fish thrashing about in shallow water. Whilst this may not be a

Fighting a fish by hand. Note the position of the rod.

problem to the boat angler, the chances are that on a short line the fish has a greater chance of breaking the leader because there is not so much stretch, and everything is that much more critical. One significant factor is that the closer the fish is to the angler, the less time the angler has to react.

I always try to dissuade my fish from jumping. This probably stems from my early coarse-fishing days when I was told to keep the fish under the water in order not to disturb the swim. Many

Netting a fish. Note that the rod is held high, and the fish is on its side.

trout gain their freedom during a jump, so I never rush my fish to the surface, being content to play them steadily at a reasonable distance from the bank where they have a good depth of water.

Experienced anglers often have a good laugh at novice anglers attempting to net their fish. The comedy usually starts when the angler tries to net a fish that has not been played out. The angler does not have complete control as both rod and line are being held in one hand while he stretches forward with the net. Then follows a frantic chase with the trout always in the lead.

Too many fish are lost at the net because they have not been fully played out. They frantically try to regain their freedom when they enter shallow water, and the silhouette of the angler and the splash of the net make things worse. Always play your trout out until it lays on its side. It can then be drawn over the submerged net and lifted from the water. Always net your own trout unless you know and trust the skill of the angler who is offering to help you.

A problem does occur if you are using a long leader for nymph fishing. Leaders can be up to 20 feet long, sometimes even more. Here again I do not like to retrieve the leader inside the rod rings until the fish is fully played out. The use of the needle knot to join a butt to the fly line provides a very slim joint which can pass easily to and fro through the rod rings. However, I prefer to let the fly line take the strain of passing through the tip ring where there is the highest possibility of wear and friction. When the fish is played out I retrieve enough line to make the netting procedure both comfortable and efficient.

It is common sense to bring a fish to the net as quickly as possible. The more time that the fish spends in the water, the more chance it has to escape. The small hole made in the jaw by the hook can grow rapidly during the fight, and a sudden turn or the slightest amount of slack line can result in a lost fish.

However, one of the major pleasures we experience when fishing is the fight of a good trout, and I do not like to see a fish hauled to the bank. In fact I sometimes wonder whether such anglers get any enjoyment from fishing at all. Remember that fighting a fish too hard can result in broken lines, broken hooks or loss caused by pulling the hook out of the fish. Balance and feel are the key to getting the highest percentage of fish on to the bank.

Chapter 14

Care of your tackle

Having invested a considerable sum of money in your fishing tackle it is necessary to maintain it properly in order to ensure that it has a long life and is fully dependable. Luckily, fly fishing tackle is basically simple, and maintenance takes only a short time, but it is certainly necessary if you are not to be let down.

Flies

You cannot maintain flies as such, but you can ensure that the hooks remain in good condition once you have either purchased or tied the fly. Hooks are prone to rust which causes weakening of the hook itself, and dulling of the point. Make sure that your fly box is not lined with a material which holds water. Keep the box in a well-ventilated cupboard when you are not fishing, especially during the winter. Discard immediately any flies with rusty hooks or any flies which show signs of discoloration which may be an indication of rust under the dressing. Carry a small sharpening stone to keep a good point on the hook, and check the hook whenever you snag on the back cast or during the retrieve. Also check your hook should you ever lose a fish. You may well find that the point is blunt, or the hook has been partially straightened. If you strike at fish which shed the hook immediately it is possible that the point of the hook may have broken off at the barb. Always try and select hooks with a shallow-cut barb, as hooks with deeper cuts may prove to be weaker.

Leaders

Many anglers believe that nylon monofilament lasts for ever; many more have found that this is not the case. Nylon is susceptible to light and heat, and will deteriorate surprisingly rapidly if it is not kept in suitable conditions. Most of the monofilament sold in the UK is manufactured in Germany. It is firstly stocked by wholesalers, then retailers before you buy it. There is no way of telling how old the retailer's stock is, but avoid line that has been kept near a shop window or over a heat source such as a radiator. Inspect the line in the shop by uncoiling a yard or two, then pulling it between your thumb and index finger. If a white powder is left on your fingers, the line is beginning to deteriorate. Refuse it.

Naturally enough, the line is your responsibility once you have purchased it, so you must do your best to look after it bearing in mind what has been said previously. I use both continuously tapered leaders and knotted leaders which I make up myself. However, I gauge my purchases carefully, usually buying 25- or 50-metre spools, so that by the end of the season I have very little line left. What is left I throw away, and start each new season with a new supply of line.

Bear in mind that knots can reduce the breaking strain of monofilament by up to 40 per cent. The worst knot is probably the granny knot which, as often as not, is also the common wind knot. Undo those wind knots as soon as you see them, or tie on a new leader.

Fly lines

Fly lines are fairly expensive today, and in order to ensure that they give you good service they do have to be maintained regularly. I think it only necessary to deal with PVC-coated lines here, as very few stillwater anglers will use silk lines.

You will see when you purchase a fly line that it is loosely coiled. This is the only sensible way to pack them; but fly lines do have a memory, and it is necessary to remove the memory before putting the line on the reel if you want to avoid kinking. I have found that the best way to remove the coils and to stretch the line is to suspend it between two posts (washing-line posts are ideal) about 30 feet apart, then hang a weight in the middle (half a house brick is about right). Leave the line for three or four hours after which time the coils will have been removed. The line can now be wound on to the reel after having been attached to the backing.

During use, the PVC coating on a fly line can be damaged in a number of ways. The most common occurrence is the line being trodden on by the angler. Try to avoid this at all costs as the coating is quite delicate. Any damage will certainly affect the qualities of a floating line.

Except when fishing, keep your lines out of the sun and away from heat sources. The plasticiser in the PVC evaporates, slowly stiffening the line and making it more susceptible to cracking. A proprietary plasticiser can now be purchased which helps keep the line supple. I apply this only when I put my lines away at the end of the season.

Floating lines require a periodic application of floatant, and it is advisable to use the floatant marketed by the line manufacturer. On no account use mucilin which may damage the fly line coating, or petroleum-based greases which will have a disastrous effect.

At the end of the season, and at regular intervals during it if your lines have a lot of use, strip them from the reel and rinse them in lukewarm soapy water to remove grit, mud, and grime from the coating. Re-grease floating lines.

Remove lines from reels at the end of the season, wash, plasticise if necessary, and store in very loose coils in a dry, cool, atmosphere. Mark the end of each double-taper line where it was attached to the leader in case you want to change the line round for next season.

Reels

Always ensure that the ratchet or check on your reel is working properly. You may think that you will never fight a fish off the reel, and the check will not be used, but the time will come when a fish will take your fly immediately after the cast and you will have to give it line. If your check is not working, a good fish can easily be lost.

Make sure that the rim of the spool does not have any rough spots to catch your fingers or cut the line.

Reels do not need much lubricant; in fact, some of the modern reels need no lubrication whatsoever. Standard reels, however, need some grease on the gearing cogs and the ratchet mechanisms. At the end of every season clear the old grease out (it is surprising how much grit and dust gets into a reel) and replace with a light smear of lubricant. Make sure however that you do not leave any lubricant anywhere near the spool or line guide where it will come into contact with the fly line.

Rods

Today's rods of glass fibre, carbon and boron take a lot of abuse, and need little maintenance. It is necessary however to check them occasionally. Rinse all reel fittings, especially the screw type, to avoid grit getting caught in the thread and seizing the fitting. Keep cork handles dry during storage otherwise they will deteriorate. A very light rub with fine sandpaper will rejuvenate the cork and ensure a good grip.

If you do happen to have an accident with the rod, check the suspect area carefully. The slightest fracture in the rod wall will cause failure under stress. It is possible to repair broken rods, but this type of work should be carried out by a good rod builder. Fractures in fine tip sections are often impossible to repair, but spare sections are usually available for the better quality rods.

Modern rods do not necessarily require a varnish coat as the materials do not naturally deteriorate. The whippings however do require protection, and should be regularly checked along with the guides throughout the season. The continuous movement of the line through the rod rings will cause wear on the stainless-steel or hardened-chrome type of guide. This wear usually takes the form of a groove which will have sharp edges. The groove will ruin the coating of a fly line, and will cut through a nylon leader in seconds. Replace worn guides as soon as you notice them with a similar type of guide, or otherwise replace all the guides with the type of your choice.

The replacing of a guide is very straightforward, and can be undertaken by the angler. Firstly cut the whippings away from the guide without touching the blank, and remove the guide. Also remove any loose varnish from the area, and very lightly sand the blank to provide a good key. Put the replacement guide into position using a thin strip of adhesive tape, and check for alignment. Using a fine whipping silk or nylon begin whipping on the blank, working towards the guide. Take care to keep the turns firm and touching. Work up over the foot of the guide towards the leg, keeping the tension even. Stop whipping four or five turns from the leg, and insert a loop of nylon with the two ends pointing away from the guide, over your whipping. Continue whipping the four or five turns over the loop, and put the end of the silk through the loop. Pull the two ends of the loop so that the whipping thread is pulled under the four or five turns of whipping and out again. Trim closely with a sharp knife.

Apply two or three coats of model aircraft dope, then two or three coats of polyurethane varnish, ensuring that you cover all the sanded area of the blank. Tippings of a different colour are applied after the guide has been whipped on.

If you are using the popular single leg guides such as the Fuji BFG, whip up the foot, and then whip a few turns behind the foot in order to lock the guide in place.

The only other maintenance that your rod requires is the regular application of a thin smear of candlewax or beeswax to the joints whether they be of the spigot or the overlap type. This will ensure a firm joint which will not twist, and will also prevent water or dirt getting into it. Always store rods in a warm, dry atmosphere, preferably hung up inside a dry rod bag.

1 Whipping the guide. Start the whipping on the blank and work up to the guide.

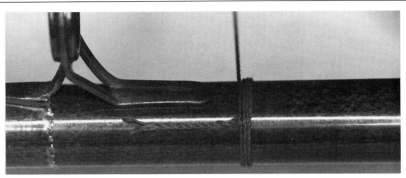

2 Insert the loop of silk under the whipping just in front of the guide frame.

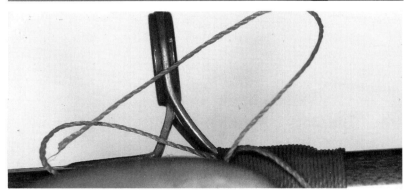

3 Continue the whipping up to the guide frame. Cut the thread and push the end through the loop.

4 Pull both ends of the loop.

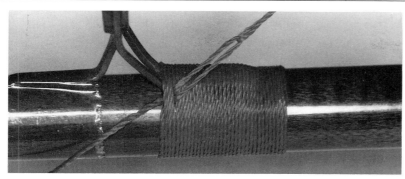

5 Continue pulling the loop so that the end of the whipping thread goes under the whipping.

6 Pull the loose end of the whipping thread under and out of the whipping.

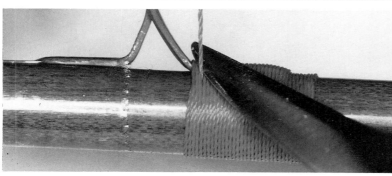

7 Hold the loose end very tightly, and cut it as near the whipping as possible.

8 When cut, the loose end will spring back under the whipping, leaving a smooth finish.

With care, your tackle will last you for many years. Rods are virtually ageless, and that is one reason for making sure that you choose the right one initially. Reels are the same, although it may be necessary to purchase replacement ratchets or checks occasionally. Fly lines of course do need to be replaced as they are subject to a lot of wear. However, it is not uncommon for a line to give five or six years of good service provided that it is looked after.

Chapter 15

How to be successful

Success in fishing, like anything else, means a certain amount of work and dedication. The majority of trout anglers catch nothing on their first trip, and very little in their first season. Success comes with practice and the acquisition of knowledge.

Knowledge is the most important item in the trout fisher's armoury. It matters not how good an angler's tackle is or how far he can cast. He will not be successful unless he has a good basic knowledge of trout-fishing techniques, and of the fishery that he is visiting. The best anglers have mastered sufficient techniques to be successful on many different waters, but they also have to be in a position to adapt their techniques to the water conditions prevailing at the time. An angler relying on the use of lures will certainly catch a lot of fish, as will the angler who relies on the use of nymphs. However, the angler who has mastered both techniques will certainly catch more, provided that he can evaluate the situation properly.

The two major problems facing an angler when he arrives at the water are: (1) Where do I fish? (2) What do I use? Many anglers show surprise when they fail to catch fish in the same place using the same method as they did on the previous day. I expect in fact that we have all experienced this nonplussed feeling, but have found it difficult to explain it away. We must therefore take a closer look at the habits of trout. We cannot think like a trout, but can at least do our best to understand the basic needs of the fish.

Firstly we must take for granted the fact that trout are interested in two things: food and sex. Some wives may find a connection here with their husbands, but we must not dwell on this. The need for food is a year-round problem, whereas the sexual urge is seasonal. (Here the connection probably ends.) The only other instinct a trout has that we are aware of is self-preservation, but as the majority of our waters do not hold predators large enough to worry trout (or if they do, they are few and far between), this part of their instinct is not so important. However, we shall return to self-preservation later.

One of the most dangerous things that an angler can do is to endow the trout with any form of intelligence. Fish are primitive life forms with an extraordinarily small brain. They will, however, be frightened by vibration, changes of light intensity caused by movement, and by flies or lures that might have pricked them in the immediate past. If they are frightened they will swim away.

On the other hand, trout can be selective regarding their choice of food, and can become preoccupied with one food form if there is enough of it about. It is therefore up to the angler to find out what the food form is, and to present an artificial accordingly.

The majority of a trout's time is therefore spent hunting for food, and they will naturally go wherever favourable food forms are available. We must forget the first two weeks of the season when all the stock fish are rushing round mouthing everything that they can lay their fins on. They do not know the difference between a Cornish Pasty and a Grey Duster, and will have a go at anything. We have to concentrate on the more natural aspects of piscine behaviour, because for most of the season we are fishing for established fish.

Each and every fishery in this country has different forms of food life in it. Buzzers can be found almost everywhere, and sedges are fairly common although, of course, there are many different species in each group. The main point that we have to consider is the effect of the weather and therefore the time of year on these life forms because this is one of the major factors that dictates the whereabouts of trout in most waters.

This 4 lb rainbow was stalked for twenty minutes before it was tempted by a damsel nymph.

Early in the season there is little surface activity among food forms. You may see the occasional hatch of buzzers on a warm evening, but if a cold wind is blowing and cooling the surface temperature of the water, the buzzers will be reluctant to hatch. Therefore it is no good fishing buzzers in the surface film unless you can see some activity there.

The hawthorn fly, a terrestrial, will make an appearance in April or May. It gets blown on to the water, and if there are sufficient numbers you can expect to see some surface activity just off the bank where the wind is blowing on to the water. It will be of little use to fish a hawthorn into the wind when the fish are taking them against the opposite bank.

Early in the season, then, we tend to fish deep. The forms of life that the trout survive on are to be found on or near the bottom. This does not mean that we have to fish lures, although early on they can be very successful, especially for newly stocked fish. You must also bear in mind that bottom-dwelling forms of life are there all the year round, so here we are talking about patterns that can be fished successfully all season.

During the summer months the water warms up, and the various food forms increase and become more active. Now we have more opportunities to use our floating lines as there are regular hatches of buzzer, sedges and, to a lesser extent, olives. Remember that buzzers can hatch over water sometimes as deep

The marrow spoon in use. This trout had eaten snail and black buzzers.

as 20 feet. Sedges, however, hatch over water normally no deeper than 12 feet. Dragonfly and damsel fly nymphs crawl or swim to the margins, and make their way up reed stems to hatch. It is therefore useful to fish a nymph pattern close in if you have disturbed a number of damsel flies when walking along the bank. I have seen trout taking adult damsels at Kennick. It appeared that the fish came out of the water and landed on the fly to drown it, then took the fly from underneath.

The weather plays a very important part in summer trout fishing. A cold wind will deter flies from hatching, and this will force the angler to fish deeper. During the day, bright sunlight will force the fish down deeper. They cannot shut their eyes or squint, so they must go deeper to avoid the bright sun. One of the major food forms, Daphnia, is affected by the light. In general, the brighter the light, the deeper the Daphnia swim. In fisheries where Daphnia is a major source of food this must be taken into serious consideration by the angler.

I well remember an evening at the Queen Mother Reservoir, Datchet. I was fishing a black lure fairly deep, but for no apparent reason I was getting take after take when only my leader was left in the water. I looked over the side of the boat, and the water was thick with Daphnia. A quick change to a smaller lure brought results, but only from the top 6 feet of water. The answer was to let the lure sink, then bring it up through the Daphnia.

As I have mentioned before, the wind plays an important part in the location of fish. The old saying, 'When the wind's in the east, the fish bite least' can hold very true. The east wind is a cold wind. It cools the surface temperature, and can stop surface activity. This may not be obvious in high summer, but in the spring and autumn a change of wind direction to the east can cause problems.

We all know that warm water is less dense than cold water, and is usually found on the surface. This warmer water can attract food forms and therefore trout as well. However, trout tend to avoid water temperatures over about 72 degrees Fahrenheit and may swim deeper or find shade. A decent ripple on the surface can reduce the temperature and scatter the sunlight, permitting the fish to remain near the surface.

In the spring a warm breeze can increase the surface temperature of the water, but as this water hits the dam or bank against which the wind is blowing it builds up the water temperature in that area. I do not think it necessary to discuss the scientific problems of thermoclines, but it is useful to know where the warmer water may be found, because if the general water temperature is cold, fish will congregate in the area which offers the best conditions for them.

Conversely, a breeze which cools the surface temperature will cause a build-up of cooler water against the bank. This may be helpful if the general water temperature is very high, but it can prove to be a less productive fishing area if temperatures are low.

I do not necessarily agree with the argument that sub-surface nymphs or dry flies should be fished into the wind because the surface drift will push food forms towards the bank. I believe that most natural food forms taken by trout are taken very close to the area where they reach the surface. After all, that is where the greatest concentration of food will be, and therefore that is the area which will attract the trout in the greatest numbers.

Hanningfield is famous for its hatches of buzzers, and I have seen buzzer shucks drifting against the bank facing the wind in such profusion that I have been tempted to put a team of buzzers amongst them. Little good it did me.

Fishing into the wind from the bank can be profitable although hard work, where waves may have dislodged nymphs from marginal growth along the bank. The fish can feed very well under these conditions, but I prefer to fish from a boat anchored upwind and cast a nymph into the cloudy water around the margins. I have found however that the trout prefer to patrol in the clear water outside the mud line.

Towards the autumn the trout go on a feeding spree to build up strength for their annual orgy (whether or not they are capable of doing it). More trout show cannibalistic tendencies at this time of the year than at any other. Small fish congregate in areas which suit them — marginal weed beds, entrances to feeder streams, and around valve towers or pilings. I really believe that the lure comes into its own then. The Church Fry, Appetiser, Baby Doll, and Muddler Minnow are probably the leading lures in this field. It is worth spending some time trying to locate fry-feeding trout rather than fishing haphazardly. Find the weed beds when the water is low or clear in the summer, and make a note of them. Remember however that although much of the surface activity will have finished, those nymphs will still be grubbing around on the bottom, and no trout will be averse to taking a good-sized nymph.

In October 1985 I fished the final of the *Angling Times* Trout League at Rutland. I had only visited the water once before, a number of years previously. The trout were heavily into fry, and the static floating fry was working well. On the practice day Steve Parton and I watched a number of large brown trout feeding on the fry. It was an amazing sight to see brownies of 6 or 7 lb leap clear of the water and land with an almighty splash then circle round to pick up the dead and stunned fry. A couple of good fish were caught, and Steve lost a trout that we did not even see, but I have never seen line stripped from a reel as quickly as Steve's was. However, these large trout were not feeding on fry all over the reservoir. Normanton bank and the dam were the areas to concentrate on. To fish a floating fry in other areas would have been a waste of time.

I mentioned earlier the trout's sense of self-preservation, and said that it was not of great significance. Having said that, it should be borne in mind that man is the trout's greatest predator, and the trout soon get to know it. Silhouettes against the skyline, heavy footfalls, bright clothing, clumsy wading and careless casting all lead to fewer trout. So take your time and take care.

Assuming that you have read the water correctly or taken good local advice, the second question now comes into play. Just what do you put on the end of your leader? It is all very well fishing in the right place, but on a strange water it can be very difficult to select a suitable fly.

Early or late in the season you may well be tempted to try a lure. This will naturally be the case if you are after one of the large carnivorous trout that have taken up deep-water residence in some of our larger fisheries. Basically your selection is fairly simple. Black, white, orange or green, plus variations involving these colours. The pattern however is a different matter, and favourite patterns vary from water to water, seemingly without any understandable reason.

The lures mentioned in Chapter 12 are good general patterns and will work most of the time. However, you will find that most waters have their own favourite patterns. The Hanningfield lure is a prime example. Trial and error is the only way to find out which lure will work except in autumn when trout may be feeding on fry, then one of the accepted patterns worked along the margins can produce spectacular results. Work systematically and thoroughly, gradually building your knowledge of the water, and you will get results.

Should the angler decide to fish imitative patterns, whether fly or nymph, his job can be made easier by means of a logical approach. Initially decide which flies or nymphs are likely to be on or in the water. For example, discard sedge patterns early on in the season. Do not fish corixa patterns if there are no corixa in the water. If damsel flies are about, then a damsel nymph may do well, as might a pheasant tail nymph. If you can see delicate sipping rises, it might well be that the fish are feeding on buzzers. Work through the colours until you get a result.

Above all, keep thinking and working logically. Try each fly or lure at different depths using a different speed of retrieve. Search the water thoroughly, then move on. Of late, many anglers seem satisfied to fish in the same place all day. This is fine so long as they are taking fish, but pointless otherwise. If for some reason the area of your choice is not suitable for the trout, they will not visit it. You cannot encourage them to the area in the same way as a coarse fisherman can. You must go and find them. Here again it is necessary to work logically and thoroughly, keeping your eyes open for any signs of fish activity.

The most valuable asset of all is local knowledge. This can only be gained by spending time on the water, and the lack of it proves a continual problem for visiting anglers. However, I have found that stillwater trout anglers are amongst the most friendly and helpful anglers that I have ever met. Fishery owners and managers must ensure that their waters produce reasonable results; a new angler going away fishless may never return. When visiting a new water I never hesitate to ask for advice from local anglers, and as far as I am aware, they have never intentionally misdirected me.

More should be done to help disabled anglers. A specially built boat in operation at Upper Tamar.

In turn, I would ask that you too help anglers visiting your water to have a successful day, and to enjoy their sport.

I cannot recommend strongly enough the advantages of joining a club. When I moved to Devon in 1982 I joined Kennick Fly Fishers, a club of about 130 members. My wife and I have received so much help from some of the members that our learning period at Kennick was reduced to about two years. This is not to say that we know *all* about Kennick; we are always learning, but we know enough to be moderately successful. Fly-tying classes, two-day fly-fishing courses, films, lectures, and competitions are an integral part of the club activities, although we must admit that much is learned over a pint at the bar after the meeting. If there is a club near you, it is certainly worth joining. Many clubs are associated with individual waters, but recently a number of clubs have been formed which do not have a 'home' water and therefore arrange trips to different fisheries.

During the winter it is worthwhile going to fly-tying classes instead of sitting at home looking forlornly at your rods. Fly-tying is a natural extension to fly fishing and gaining knowledge of the technique is very rewarding – just for that feeling of absolute smugness the first time that you hook and land a trout on a fly that you have tied yourself.

If you can afford it, a course of casting lessons will certainly pay dividends. It will save you wasting money on fisheries where you cannot reach the fish, and will also save you looking a complete novice on the bank. Let it be said however that some of our best anglers have casting styles that would make an instructor cringe. If you do have lessons, make sure that your instructor is a member of the APGAI, which is recognised as the professional body.

All in all, successful fly fishing means a certain amount of time and dedication, the ability to think both logically and thoroughly, and the ability to put your deductions into action.

I hope that this book will help you to enjoy your sport, for enjoyment is the main aim. The fish that you take home are a bonus. The feeling of fulfilment after a good day on the water is reward enough.

Appendix

One delightful thing about trout fishing is that we are always learning. Luckily we shall never know everything that there is to know, but today there is a tremendous fund of knowledge available to us all in the form of angling literature.

Regardless of whether you are a complete novice or an expert, there is always something to be gained by reading, and in some cases re-reading, a book.

Listed below are a few of the books that I regard as classics among stillwater trout fishing literature.

Books for further reading

The Pursuit of Stillwater Trout, Brian Clarke, A & C Black, 1975.
Trout Flies of Stillwater, John Goddard, A & C Black, 1979.
Reservoir Trout Fishing, Bob Church, A & C Black, 1983.
Boatfishing for Trout, Steve Parton, George Allen & Unwin, 1983.
The Super Flies of Stillwater, John Goddard, Ernest Benn, 1977.
Fly Dressing, David Collyer, David & Charles, 1975.
Fly Dressing Vol. II, David Collyer, David & Charles, 1981.
Fly Casting, James Tomlinson, A & C Black, 1984.

Useful organisations

Anglers' Co-operative Association
Midland Bank Chambers
Westgate
Grantham NG1 7LE   Tel: 0476 61008

The British Field Sports Society
59, Kennington Road
London SE1 7PZ   Tel: 01-828 4742

Country Landowners' Association
16, Belgrave Square
London SW1   Tel: 01-235 0511

Flyfishers' Club
24, Old Burlington Street
London W1   Tel: 01-734 9229

Stillwater Trout

National Anglers' Council
11, Cowgate
Peterborough PE1 1LZ   Tel: 0733 54084

National Federation of Anglers
Halliday House
2, Wilson Street
Derby   Tel: 0332 362000

Salmon and Trout Association
Fishmongers' Hall
London EC4   Tel: 01-626 3531

Index

sinking lines, 46–51, *47*
stance, 74–5
sterile fish, 18
Stick Fly, 124
stillwater fisheries, 20–7
stocking policies, 25–7
sun glasses, 65
Sweeney Todd, 118

T

tiger trout, 17
triploids, 18
trousers, 66–7
trout, types, 11–18

V

Viva, 118

W

wading, 22
waistcoats, 65
Walker's Sedge, 130
weight forward lines, 45, 55
wet flies, 125–8
whippings, 141, *142–3*
Whiskey Fly, 118–19
Wickham's Fancy, 128
wrist straps, 73, *73*

Z

Zulu, 127